CONVICT AUSTRALIA

Extraordinary true stories of shipwrecks, riots, daring escapes and more.

JENNIFER TWEMLOW

Copyright © 2024 Jennifer Twemlow

Year: 2024

Sydney, Australia

All rights reserved. No reproduction, transmission or copy of this publication can be made without the written consent of the author in accordance with the provision of the Copyright Acts. Any person doing so will be liable to civil claims and criminal prosecution.

For Oliver

Contents

~

Introduction vii
Amphitrite 1
The *Surry* 6
Three Naked Convicts, a Kangaroo Suit and the Dog-Line 12
Thomas Drewery, An Innocent Man 20
Convict Pirates of Moreton Bay 28
Australia's First Cold Case and the Man They Couldn't Hang 37
A Daring Escape from the Road Gangs of Western Australia 43
The Audacious Plot to Rescue Six Irish Convicts from Prison 50
The Disastrous Voyage of *George III* 59
The Tea Sweetners 68
The First Fleeters and their Struggle for Food 74
The Sinking of the *Guardian* 82
The Extraordinary Story of Mary Bryant – First Fleeter, Wife and Mother 90
The Cooking Pot Riot 104
Neva – One of the Worst Shipwrecks in Australian History 110
Australia's First Bank Robbery 116
Ten Convict Pirates Seize the *Frederick* 128
Glossary 139
Bibliography 143
Acknowledgements 155
Also by Jennifer Twemlow 156

Introduction

Britain seriously underestimated the grit and determination of so many of the unwanted offenders they dumped on Australia's shores. From 1788 roughly 166,000 convicts were transported to Australia to serve out the sentences for their crimes. The following stories are the lived experiences of some of those men, women and children that were transported.

Sadly, for some, their stories ended before they even reached the shores of Australia, as many died from disease, poor diet, and overcrowded, unventilated conditions below the decks. Although there was a high success rate of getting the convicts to Australia, a few ships were wrecked enroute. Their epic struggles for survival as the ships slowly broke apart in the giant ocean swells are retold within the pages of this book. So too are chilling plots of rebellion and riots as convicts pushed back against cruel overseers and power-hungry men in authority. There are also stories of truly extraordinary escapes that were clever and well-planned out, showing strength of character, determination and will.

The *Convict Australia* Podcast has been a platform to rediscover this significant period of Australian history and celebrate these men, women and children. These are their stories — some tragic, some heroic, some inspiring and some so unjust and avoidable, but all insightful. I believe it's important to keep these stories alive to better understand our past and the people that shaped our nation.

Amphitrite

Between 1788 and 1868, hundreds of ships transported roughly 166,000 convicts to Australia. Travelling to Australia by ship meant spending months at sea and the risks were extremely high. Each ship embarking on this journey to the other side of the world would have faced a range of dangers such as fire, bad weather, high seas, disease, seasickness and cramped, unsanitary conditions just to name a few. These were real fears, but up until 1833 over 70,000 convicts had been transported to the colonies safely. Many had been lost to disease, ill-treatment and mutiny or suspected plans of mutiny, but none of the convict transportation ships had been lost to shipwreck.

Being shipwrecked was a dangerous prospect. There weren't enough lifeboats to carry everyone on board and few knew how to swim – including the crew! If they were lucky to make it to shore, there was no way to communicate back home that they needed rescuing. If they were stranded somewhere away from civilisation their life depended on catching the eye of a passing ship. Survivors were faced with the very real prospect of a slow death due to starvation and exposure to the elements.

Surprisingly, only five ships transporting convicts from the UK to Australia were shipwrecked. The first, and perhaps the most heart-rending, was the *Amphitrite*. The *Amphitrite* was a very small vessel compared to the other transport ships and one of the oldest. It was a strange choice for such a long voyage.

The master and part-owner of the ship was 33-year-old

John Hunter who had eight years of experience of being in command of ships under his belt. The surgeon chosen for the voyage was James Forrester. Forrester was in disgrace for his previous voyage on *Southworth* where he had dispensed all his medicine without logging the details in his journal. Sir William Burnett had warned: *'Inform Mr Forrester that I am by no means satisfied with the reasons he has given for inserting so few cases in this Journal, and that if anything of a similar nature should again occur, the certificate to enable him to obtain the remainder of his pay etc will not be granted.'* His appointment was an opportunity for Forrester to redeem himself. Along for the ride was his wife who had been granted permission to travel with him. This was highly unusual, and it is assumed that they had plans to settle in New South Wales.

Roughly 106 female convicts, their 12 children, a crew of 16, along with Forrester and his wife boarded the ship. Most of the convicts were from all over Britain, with a large portion taken from Newgate Prison. Elizabeth Fry, the quaker humanitarian, had armed many of them with bibles, sewing kits and a fresh set of clothing before boarding. Once below deck the female convicts and their children were assigned a berth. Each sleeping berth was shared by three girls and a child if they had any. This amounted to roughly 18 inches each – quite a luxury for some. The height between the decks was horrendous for most though, as it was only five and a half feet and less than five under the beams. The average height of the women was 5 feet 1 ¾ inches, with the tallest being 5 feet 8 ½ inches.

It was the surgeon's role to look after the prisoners and keep them occupied and in line. The boatswain, John Owen, vented his frustration in a comment: *'The women had the range of the ship. The doctor let them go where they liked: he never took any notice, if they did not make a riot.'* Owen was so exasperated with the surgeon's lack of control that he frequently had to take matters into his own hands, resorting to throwing water over the women who wouldn't leave the crew alone to do their work. The language and behaviour of some of the women shocked him so much he described it as *'outrageous and disgusting beyond anything the men had ever heard.'*

Forrester had brought a punishment box with him and set it up on the top deck. The box stood upright in the sun like a vertical coffin. Before the ship had even left Woolwich a prisoner had been confined in the box. It was extremely narrow, making it impossible to sit down and very difficult to bend the knee. The height of the box was relatively low, and many prisoners had to hunch their shoulders and press their chin down on their chest to fit inside. For the person locked inside it was like being buried alive. It was painfully hot, with only a few holes at the top to prevent suffocation. The prisoner was often forced to endure hours of this and feared that they may have been forgotten about. If they screamed a bucket of water was poured over it. This punishment subdued even the most troublesome prisoner.

The *Amphitrite* left Woolwich on 25 August in 1833 at a time of year that should have been ideal. However, they had only been sailing for a day when they ran into a fierce summer gale. Instead of turning back they decided to press on. On 30 August conditions worsened and the small ship struggled in treacherous waves, fierce winds, and poor visibility. Despite the best efforts of the crew to keep the small vessel away from the French coastline, it grounded in a sandbank three quarters of a mile from shore. It was low tide, so Hunter dropped the anchor to await the incoming tide. He was certain that the ship would float off when the tide turned – the locals knew better. They had seen the sands of Boulogne claim vessels far stronger than the *Amphitrite*.

Meanwhile, thousands of spectators gathered on the beach to witness the stranded ship. A pilot boat set out to rescue them, but Hunter, believing that they were not in serious danger, declined the offer and sent them away. He also didn't want to risk the women being able to escape into France.

When the pilot boat returned to shore, a French sailor by the name of Pierre Henin tied a light rope to himself and swam for about an hour to the ship. He was concerned that the commander of the pilot boat hadn't been able to convey the critical situation the ship was in to the master in English. When he finally reached the ship and asked them to throw down a line so he might save them, they refused him too. Flabbergasted and utterly spent, he was left with no choice but to swim back to shore.

The rescue attempts began to sow seeds of doubt in the mind of Forrester, and he ordered the boatswain to lower the longboat. However, Forrester's wife refused to share a boat with the convicts, so the idea was abandoned. By now panic had set in and the women and children who had been locked into the hold below had broken free, their cries of anguish and distress carried on the wind to be heard by the French who watched on helplessly.

Hours later when the tide finally came in, it battered the *Amphitrite* breaking it in two. Within a few minutes the ship had collapsed to pieces. Everyone on board fell into the water, desperately scrambling to grab hold of pieces of the wreckage. By 2 a.m. it was all over. By morning, the beach was littered with dead bodies and parts of the wreck. None of the convicts or their children survived. Neither did the

Master, Forrester or his wife. Only three crew members managed to make it to shore clutching their piece of the torn apart ship to keep themselves afloat.

Tragically, 133 people were drowned in total. Only 82 bodies were ever retrieved. The bodies were put into a mass grave nearby and today there stands a memorial pillar. Perhaps the saddest image of this senseless accident, was the body of a woman who was washed ashore clutching her child in her arms. She was holding on so tightly that her arms couldn't be pried apart.

The *Surry*

It had been an exceptionally bitter, cold winter, the Thames freezing over with what would be the last of the frost fairs. Thomas Blade, along with his friend Richard and 198 other convict men, grudgingly made his way up the gangway. The brisk dry air and biting wind ripped through him as he shuffled onto the deck before filing down into the gloomy depths of the ship. His hazel eyes adjusting to the dark he peered around the space, taking in what was to be his home for the next few months. When all were aboard it would take a few more weeks of loading up the vessel with provisions in preparation for its long arduous journey to the other side of the world. The year was 1814.

Thomas was 34 years old, with light brown hair, a pale complexion and stood at 5 feet, 4 inches tall. He and Richard had been caught stealing hams from a shop in East Smithfield five months prior. Despite both pleading their innocence, they had been found guilty and sentenced to death, which had later been commuted to transportation for life. To his relief, in the months leading up to his transportation his beloved wife Sarah had been granted passage on the *Broxbornebury*. Their three children, as well as his eldest child to his first wife, would be travelling with her. The *Broxbornebury* was a three-decker sailing ship that, along with his family and other free settlers, would be carrying over 100 convict women and some cargo to New South Wales. When the weather took on a slightly milder feel towards the end of February it was decided it was a good time to go. On 22 February the

Surry, along with the *Broxbornebury* set sail for New South Wales.

As they pulled further and further away from land the routine on the *Surry* ebbed and flowed. The convict men were divided into nine groups with either 20 or 21 men in each. Another 14 men were given duties to perform and were able to move about the ship freely. Each division took turns to come up from below deck. It was an opportunity for Thomas to seek out the *Broxbornebury* and possibly catch a glimpse of his family. It was also a chance to breathe the fresh crisp air deep into his lungs and feel the spray on his face before returning to the claustrophobic confines down below. During these rotations their area was washed and fumigated. Vinegar, soap, and mustard were issued for cleaning their spaces and themselves. Tuesdays and Fridays were wash days. On Sundays they were read a divine service and enjoyed their ration of wine.

Life on board continued uneventfully for Thomas until 7 March when the surgeon confirmed that a convict named John Stopgood, had a sure case of Typhus, or gaol fever as it was commonly termed then. Typhus is a highly infectious disease caused by lice and flea bites. The lice would defecate on the human as it feasted on their skin. The sufferer would scratch the bites and inadvertently get faecal matter into their wound. This bacteria led to headaches, a violent rash of red spots and a harsh fever. These lice would thrive in dirty, overcrowded areas with people who could not regularly wash themselves or their clothing. Prisons offered conditions that were perfect for the incubation of Typhus which thus earned the nickname of 'gaol fever'.

Five days later, on 12 March, John Ranson became the first to die on board of the disease, which triggered a ripple effect, one man dying after the other at an alarming rate.

The convicts were now split into eight divisions and kept to the same rotation. The journals of the surgeon were almost perfunctory, and although there is mention of his attention to fumigating and cleansing the ship, there is no mention of ventilation. At no time were all the convicts let up on the deck at the same time, nor was their bedding brought up on deck for a thorough airing. When it was Thomas' turn to go up on deck, he was no longer able to see the *Broxbornebury*. The two ships had parted ways at some point. He could only hope that the disease had not spread on the ship his wife and children were on.

On 11 April they sailed into Rio De Janeiro where they stocked up on beef, fruit and vegetables. The captain even brought on board tobacco, coffee and sugar for the convicts to purchase if they had the means. They stayed in Rio for 10 days, then departed on 21 April.

The fumigation continued. Thomas rigorously cleaned his bedding and sleeping area to try and prevent further contagion. From 24 May all mention of convicts receiving divine service stops. By this time the disease had spread from the convicts to members of the crew, soldiers, the captain and even the surgeon himself. The last recorded death is on 9 June when Aaron Jackson dies of fever, but the deaths continued.

The *Surry* was now in a desperate state. With 12 seaman, two mates and the captain seriously ill there was no one to navigate her safely to shore. On 26 July the *Surry* was limping along, hugging the coastline just off the Shoalhaven when the *Broxbornebury* approached. The timing couldn't have been better. A very relieved Thomas Raine, the last standing junior officer, relayed their dilemma and implored Captain Pilcher for assistance. The following day, a seaman, by the name of Nash, voluntarily boarded the struggling ship and took the reins. Captain Paterson died that same day. Perhaps he had been holding on but finally succumbed when he knew that the ship was in safe hands.

Nash guided the *Surry* into Port Jackson and anchored on 29 July. When authorities took in the state of the convicts, they were shocked to see how sick and dirty they were. Asked why they hadn't washed with soap, they replied, *'There was none, it was all expended.'* The soap was later found with a list of goods for sale.

The ship was immediately put into quarantine and the sick sent to camps on the North Shore. Thomas was desperate to see his family but was not allowed to leave the camp. The authorities were ready for them. Tents had been set up and every precaution was taken to stop the further spread of the disease. Advertisements were published in the *Sydney Gazette* warning the public to stay away from the camps and anyone breaking these rules would be severely punished.

On 13 August another announcement was made in the *Sydney Gazette* that the ship was now free of Typhus and was released from quarantine. However, Thomas and the rest of the people who travelled by the *Surry* wouldn't be released from quarantine for a further two weeks. On 31 August they left the quarantine camp and were brought to Sydney. They had left London after a brutal winter only to arrive in the dead of Australia's winter, cold, weak and having survived an emotional toll.

Governor Lachlan Macquarie employed the services of Surgeon William Redfern to conduct an investigation into the heavy death toll on board the *Surry* and two other ships transporting convicts to Australia at that time. Redfern had been transported to the colonies as a convict but had earned himself a pardon. He became the trusted family doctor to

Macquarie's family. He even helped deliver Macquarie's son into the world, so he was Macquarie's natural choice to lead the investigation.

Redfern reviewed what the convicts had been wearing, their diet, how much fresh air they were allowed, and the care given by the surgeon. He also examined the surgeon's journals. He concluded that *'the poison was generated by the close confinement of the convicts in the prison. It diffused its malignant influence through every part of the ship and spared none who came within the sphere of its action.'*

On 1 October of that same year Macquarie wrote to the commissioners of the transport board. *'The Mortality, which has been the Consequence, is very great, 36 Convicts died, as also the Captain of the Ship, the first and second Mates, the Boatswain and Six Seamen, besides 1 Serjeant and three Privates of the Military Detachment: In all Fifty Persons. I have much reason to apprehend that this destructive Disease originated in the mismanagement of two of the unfortunate Sufferers, namely the Captain and Surgeon, whose Duty it was equally to have caused the Convicts to be brought more frequently and in greater numbers on Deck, than it appears they thought proper to authorize.'*

William Redfern's report brought about a massive change to the way convicts were treated on their voyage out to Australia. What happened to the people on the *Surry* was a lesson to all. Thomas Raine, the junior officer, was promoted to Captain and sailed the *Surry* on five more voyages. This horrific experience shaped Raine to become a very caring and responsible Captain who treated those in his charge humanely. For this reason, he earned himself the commendation of Governor Lachlan Macquarie.

As for Thomas Blade, after months apart, he was finally reunited with his family. He was given new slop clothing and issued a Ticket of Leave. Unfortunately, he died in January 1815 when a squall upturned the boat he was in. All passengers drowned. His wife Sarah was pregnant at the time. In July that year she gave birth to their son and named him Thomas.

Three Naked Convicts, a Kangaroo Suit and the Dog-Line

∽

The Tasman Peninsula was chosen for its remote location. A place of banishment that was thought to be impossible to escape from. For this reason, repeat absconders and some of the most troublesome offenders were sent there. It soon developed a reputation as a place worse than death with its harsh psychological punishments, back-breaking tasks, and cruel overseers. It was also chosen as a place to harness and exploit the peninsula's rich environment. There were two main convict outposts – Port Arthur and the coal mines at Plunkett Point.

Port Arthur began as a timber station back in 1830. as there was an abundance of enormous eucalyptus, blue gum, stringybark and swamp gum trees. This job was a form of physical punishment. Convicts trudged into the forest where they felled huge trees, cut and trimmed them into logs and then had to drag or carry them back to the sawpits. The 70 odd men forced to carry the logs back became known as the centipede gang. A convict, Linus Miller, complained *'We were allowed to rest only once on the way, and when we reached the settlement, I was nearer dead than alive.'* Thomas Lempiere, the Assistant Commissary General, claimed that Port Arthur was known as the *'Earthly Hell.'*

But perhaps the worst job was down in the dark, dank coal mines at Plunkett Point. The air was heavy with black coal dust and there was little ventilation. The convicts spent an eight-hour shift 300 feet down extracting the coal. They were hunched over as the roof was too low for them to stand. It was so damp in the tunnels that the lamp would frequently go out leaving them in pitch blackness. The work was hard and unrelenting and if they didn't meet their daily quota of 25 tons they could be thrown into one of the four underground solitary confinement cells. The coal mines were a popular dumping ground for repeat offenders and held up to 600 prisoners. They slept in overcrowded huts. Reverend Henry Phibbs Fry visited and remarked, *'They worked without any other clothing than their trousers, and perspired profusely ... I contemplated the naked figures, faintly perceptible in the gloom, with feelings of horror. Such a scene is not to be forgotten.'*

Refusing to work only led to severe floggings, heavy leg irons and solitary confinement. However, over time, authorities moved away from physical punishments and embraced psychological punishments. Offenders were thrown into the Separate Prison where they were kept apart from other prisoners and in total silence. They were stripped of their names and referred to by their number which could be found on their uniform. They were strictly not permitted to speak unless it was to a guard or a clergyman and only for very essential reasons. When they left their cell, a hood was placed over their heads that had slits for their eyes. If they broke the rules, they were thrown into the dark cells that totally blocked out all light. Time in the dark cells could last up to three days and they were only given bread and water.

The Tasman Peninsula, with its towering sea cliffs, was surrounded by ocean with the exception of one tiny strip of land which had been named Eaglehawk Neck. It was like a bridge connecting one peninsula to the other. This stretch of land was only about 60 metres wide. It was recognised as an easy point to prevent escapees from getting to the mainland, so authorities made it a formidable place to pass. They started by posting guards there. They built huts and sentry boxes which sporadically dotted the area, and guards regularly patrolled it with their loaded guns. Every effort was made to make the pass impenetrable. Lamps were strategically placed along the road using whale oil to keep them alight. Seashells were collected and scattered along the path to help illuminate the passage even further.

However, they soon discovered that having the sound of the surf crashing on the east side of the Neck made it difficult to hear anyone approaching. John Peyton Jones of the 63rd Regiment came up with the idea of enlisting the help of watch dogs. If anyone dared to approach, the dogs would bark and snarl alerting the guards. The dogs were given ferocious names and rumours were spread about their viciousness and ability to tear a person to pieces to deter any convicts going anywhere near the pass. The dogs were chained at different spots, making a line along the neck, but their chains were long enough to meet the next dog making it impossible to get past them. The strip became known as the dog-line.

The only other way to get off the Tasman Peninsula was by swimming past Eaglehawk Neck, so they built platforms in the sea at regular intervals and stationed a dog on each. Guards would have to row out to them daily to deliver their rations of one pound of meat and bread per day – the same rations that were given to convicts. If anyone tried to swim past the dogs, they would bark and alert the guards.

Authorities also circulated stories that the waters were shark-infested and helped the stories along by throwing offal into the water in the hope of attracting sharks to the area. But despite their efforts, authorities underestimated the convicts' desperation to escape the 'earthly hell' as many knowingly risked their lives to get across. A slim chance at freedom was more appealing than another day in hell. Most escape attempts were done in the surf, but there was one man who made his attempt on land.

George Hunt, or Billy as he liked to be called, bolted into the bush, fighting his way through the thick brush, desperate to put as much distance between himself and the settlement at Port Arthur as he could. He was 27 years old at the time, 5 feet 6 inches tall with brown hair, grey eyes and large pockmarks above his right eyebrow. His tattooed arms pushed the branches out of the way as he moved deeper and deeper into the bush.

He'd been transported to the colony for stealing. The night he was arrested had been a cool evening in September 1824. He had been sauntering down the busy cobbled streets of Smithfield in London when he spotted a well-dressed man by the name of John Gilbert. Billy had quietly sidled up to Mr Gilbert and slipped his hand into the gentleman's pocket. Unfortunately, Mr Gilbert felt something, swung around and saw his handkerchief drop from Billy's hand. Later in court, Billy pleaded, *'I know nothing of it. I could have got away, but knew myself innocent.'* The court found him guilty and sentenced him to 14 years transportation. He was only 20 years old at the time.

Billy knew that his only hope of living a life of freedom was to escape from the peninsula. Stories of the many failed attempts to cross the dog-line regularly circulated the settlement. Billy had to think of something extraordinary if he was going to get across. Something that no other person had attempted before. And just like that, an idea popped into his head, and he formed a plan on how to execute it.

Kitted out in a big kangaroo skin, Billy boldly stepped out into the open and began hopping along the Neck. Two hungry guards faced with another long and monotonous shift on duty, surveyed the narrow strip of land. When they spotted the giant kangaroo hopping their way, one guard exclaimed *'I think I will have a shot at that boomer'*. When Billy heard this, he quickly shed the kangaroo skin and exclaimed *'Don't shoot, I am only Billy Hunt'*. Despite this close call, Billy went on to make many more escape attempts and earned himself a range of punishments. At the end of his time Billy had been charged with at least 64 offences and had received a total of 1,800 days in leg irons, 625 lashes and spent 131 days in solitary confinement.

Another attempt to pass the Neck was made at the peak of its security and this time successfully. Martin Cash and his two mates, Lawrence Kavanagh and George Jones crouched behind bushes surveying the Neck. Cash was a notorious runaway, and this wasn't his first attempt at crossing the Neck. He had previously managed to make it through the surf but was captured on the other side halfstarved and in a weakened state. He had been promptly returned to Port Arthur.

Martin Cash was described in the *Sydney Gazette* as a *'tall powerful man, and an excellent bushman'*. He was said to have been 6 feet tall with curly carroty hair and red whiskers, a ruddy complexion and remarkably long feet making him a swift runner. When the sun had slipped beneath the horizon, Cash, Kavanagh and Jones began readying themselves to make their move. Cash described the scene: *'we could see the line literally swarming with constables'*.

Stripping off their clothing, the three convict men silently waded into the water with their clothing bundled and fastened to their heads. It was pitch black, they only had the light of the moon to guide them. They dragged their legs through the heaving swell trying to balance themselves. As each surge picked them up, they struggled to find their footing and found themselves being pushed further apart from one another. Cash soon lost sight of his friends. Suddenly a wave crashed over his head sending him tumbling. Scrambling to plant his feet back on the sandy bottom and keep his head above the water, Cash released his grip on his bundle of clothing and they disappeared into the rolling swell. Realising it was futile to try and look for it in the dark he pushed on.

In the freezing cold water, alone in the dark, being slammed repeatedly by wave after wave, he strained his eyes to spot his friends. He must have feared that they had drowned or been attacked by sharks. Moving closer to shore he faintly heard the sound of voices in the distance. He inched closer and closer, careful not to alert them of his presence by making any splashing sounds. To his relief, he recognised the voices as his two friends. He heard Jones say to Kavanagh *'Martin's drowned'*.

Once he had reached the shore, Cash carefully made his way through the dark up to where his friends were. He was completely naked and so happy to hear that both of them had made it across. Deciding to play a joke on them he crept up to where they were and leapt out in front of them. Jones and Kavanagh jumped from fright, but once they realised it was Cash, and that he was stark naked just as they were, they burst into laughter.

Once recovered, the men began the tough journey through the thick bush. Traipsing through the undergrowth with only the moon to light their path proved difficult. The further they went, the more dense the bush became. As they jostled through the shrubbery their naked bodies became so lacerated that they decide to stop and wait until daylight so they could find an easier path.

The following morning, they set off again and carefully pushed through the brush. They were shivering from the cold and feeling completely vulnerable. Eventually they came upon a small hut. Martin was already familiar with it. He knew that prisoners who were nearing the completion of their sentences were stationed there with only the one overseer. The convicts were sent there to work on the roads in the immediate area.

As they crept up to the hut, Kavanagh reached for an axe that was leaning against the wall adjacent to the door. Raising it above his head he motioned for the other two to follow him, and all at once, the men burst through the door. Cash recalled, *'I shall never forget the look of horror and amazement with which we were regarded by the unfortunate man inside, who, upon seeing three naked men rushing into the hut, one of whom was brandishing an axe, resigned himself to his fate, standing transfixed, with his mouth and eyes opened, appearing to be in a perfect state of bewilderment.'*

Before the overseer could react, they had him tied to a post and began ransacking the hut. The first thing the men grabbed were clothing and boots. They hurriedly thrust their arms and legs through the material which felt warm and protective against their cool, scratched skin. After sliding their sore feet into the boots, they raided the food supplies, greedily filling sacks with flour, bread, fresh beef, tea, and sugar. They also grabbed a steel flint and tinder box so they would be able to warm themselves by a fire and enjoy hot meals. They had everything they would need to survive in the bush for the foreseeable future. Slinging the sacks over their shoulders they fled into the bush.

The story of their daring escape quickly circulated throughout the community giving hope to their fellow convicts. Thanks to the stolen loot, Cash, Kavanagh and Jones were able to avoid capture for many months. During that time, they replenished their supplies by raiding properties of well-to-do settlers and robbing mail coaches and inns. To authorities they were known as Cash and Co, a gang of troublesome criminals, but to the general public they were the gentlemen bushrangers that stole from the rich without the use of unnecessary violence.

Over time, a growing community was living and working at the Neck, but in November 1873 it was closed down. Soon the buildings fell into disrepair and all that is left to mark this historic location is a bronze sculpture of a savage looking dog chained to a barrel and a cut through the sand dunes. There also remains one of the Officers' Quarters dating back to 1832 which has been restored and turned into a museum. It tells the story of the dog line and the history of Eaglehawk Neck.

Thomas Drewery, An Innocent Man

It was a colder than average August day in 1845 when a man strolled into an inn in Wakefield of West Yorkshire, England. The lunch time rush was just starting to die down when the man struck up a conversation with the waitress. He orders a bottle of lemonade and enquires if there is a horse and gig he can hire for the day. He explains he has business in Stanley, a town about three or four miles away and should be back by seven or eight that evening. The man drains his bottle of lemonade as the groom prepares the horse and gig. The brown mare stands at roughly 14 hands high and as the man steps up onto the two-wheeled gig, the waitress and groom ask for his details. He tells them his name is Thomas Drewery, of Hull, thus setting in motion a series of events that would change the lives of many.

The man's real name was John Webster. He was from Newcastle upon Tyne and worked as a grocer. He had caught the train up that day and randomly selected the inn. After securing his horse and gig he road past Stanley and headed back to Newcastle where a week later he sold the gig at auction and exchanged the horse for another one at Newcastle fair. Around the time Webster was gleefully pocketing the money for the gig, the real Thomas Drewery of Hull was having irons slapped on his wrists and was being led to the watchhouse.

Thomas Drewery was a young man of about 23 years of age. He was happily married to a woman named Elizabeth and the pair had two young children together. He had a respectable job as a druggist in a chemist store in Hull that was streets away from where he was born. In July 1845 Thomas headed to Leeds to have a much-deserved holiday with friends. However, that abruptly ended on 12 August when he and his friend Abraham Wilkinson returned to York and Thomas was seized by police.

Thomas was kept locked up until his trial a month later. His case was heard at the Quarter Sessions at Wakefield Court House. The prosecution had three witnesses on the day but Thomas didn't have the funds to find and pay witnesses to come to his trial, so he just had his good friend Abraham to stand up for him. But surely that was all he needed? He was an innocent man after all. Once the jury heard Abraham testify that he had been in his company on the day in question the charges would be dropped? Sadly, this wasn't to be the case.

One by one the three witnesses for the prosecution stood up and told the jury what they'd seen. All three were employees of the inn. Two swore an oath that the man they had seen was indeed the man standing before them. However, the waitress, Jane Armitage, who had spent the most time talking to the man who hired the horse, wasn't one hundred percent sure it was him. She thought it was him. It certainly looked a lot like him, but she wouldn't swear to it. There was that tiny niggling doubt.

When it was Abraham's turn to get up, he confidently explained to the jury that it could not possibly be the same man, as Thomas had been with him day and night since he arrived in July in Leeds – a town 10 miles away. So, it would have come as quite a shock when the judge handed down the verdict of guilty. Thomas had been so sure that the truth would set him free and return him to his beloved family. However, the jury just wouldn't believe one man – a friend at that – over two credible witnesses. There was no appeal system. Once a person was found guilty that was it.

Thomas was shuffled between York Castle and Milbank Prison, one festering prison to the other, before being sent onto Pentonville Prison. He did not give up hope and was determined to fight for his innocence. He decided to write as many letters as he could to whoever would listen to try and get the case reheard; he now had a lot of time on his hands, and he planned to use it productively. He couldn't bear the thought of what might become of his beloved Elizabeth and their two children. Without him and his steady wage from the Chemist they would have absolutely no means by which to live. He shuddered at the very thought. Spurred into action he started writing letters to people he thought might be able to help them. The only problem was Pentonville Prison had strict rules and one of them was that prisoners could only receive one letter every six months! And only one visitor every six months!

Meanwhile his wife and friends approached a solicitor by the name of Mr Sidebottom for help, even though they didn't have the means to pay him. Sidebottom agreed to represent Thomas and fight for his release if he believed him to be innocent. He set about reading the facts of the case and made his own inquiries. Sidebottom travelled to Leeds to track down more witnesses and found four credible people who were willing to testify that they had seen Thomas at the time of the robbery. Armed with this knowledge, Sidebottom agreed to take up the case and had the new witnesses write up affidavits supporting Thomas' alibi. Sidebottom presented these affidavits along with a letter he had written on behalf of Thomas' wife Elizabeth to the Home Office, pleading with them to re-examine the case and overturn Thomas' sentence.

Sidebottom eagerly awaited a letter from the Home Office and when it arrived, he tore it open with haste. But his exuberance turned to disappointment as he read from Sir James Graham *'that to release or acquit a prisoner upon evidence corroboratory of alibi, pleaded at the trial, was without precedent!'* Sidebottom couldn't believe what he was reading! He was outraged that the system he had spent his adult life studying and practising, the very system that he believed in passionately, could let an innocent man serve time for a crime he didn't commit. It was almost too much to bear. This was the turning point that made Sidebottom determined to see Thomas' sentence overturned, to set this man free no matter what the cost.

He personally sought out an interview with Sir Walter C James, member for Hull and persuaded him to write a letter to the Home Office in regards to Thomas' case. Sir James agreed to write the letter requesting that the matter be brought to the attention of Her Majesty the Queen for mitigation of the sentence. They received their reply on 27 April 1846. The response read:

'Sir James Graham has read the letter, and looked at the several papers before submitted to him, on behalf of the prisoner. Sir James Graham continues of the same opinion as before, namely, that he would not be warranted in advising a mitigation of the sentence in this case. Sir James Graham has seen the full report of the evidence at the trial of the prisoner, who was defended by Counsel, and his defence was an alibi. Fresh declarations are now submitted to Sir James Graham's consideration with a view to strengthen the alibi set up at the trial which the jury could not have believed. But these declarations have not been made upon oath, nor have they been submitted to cross-examination. Sir James Graham can not, therefore , consider them as entitled to weight of legitimate

evidence. I am directed to add that Sir James Graham has fully considered the case and sees no ground for deciding the propriety either of the verdict or the judgement'.

At this point, most people would have given up, but not Sidebottom. He approached another member for parliament and convinced him to also send a letter to the Home Office. Unfortunately, this was rejected too. Sidebottom had exhausted every avenue and to his utter frustration did not think he could proceed any further. All his efforts had been played out in the local newspapers and something good had come of it. The story had drummed up sympathy for Thomas and his family and one kind lady living in Regents Park wrote to Elizabeth. She said she had been following the case and expressed her deepest sympathies and told her she had left her £2 with the editor of the *Morning Post*. She hoped that her gift would set an example and other people would follow her lead. And it did! Once the papers published news of her kind donation money started to flow in.

Unfortunately, Thomas' time had come for transportation. On 2 June 1847 the *Joseph Soames* set sail for Tasmania with Thomas onboard. Thomas and his family and friends must have felt despair, all sense of hope for his release gone. Thoughts must have run through his head that he may never see his family again. But just as the ship loses sight of England, taking Thomas further and further away from his family and the only home he's ever known, an extraordinary turn of events occurs!

Over in Van Diemen's Land a convict turns to his mate one night and asks him if he's heard about the story of Thomas Drewery, of Hull? The name rings a bell, but he can't quite place it. As the convict listens to his mate regale the sorry tale, a feeling of dread washes over him as he realises that he was the one who stole the horse and gig! Thomas Drewery had been sentenced for a crime that he, John Webster, had committed! He couldn't believe it! He felt an overwhelming sense of horror and guilt. He decided he could not live with himself if he let another man suffer for a crime that he was guilty of.

Webster immediately started making enquiries to find out if the details were correct. The more he learnt the more he was convinced that he was guilty of the crime. So he wrote a letter in the hope of clearing Thomas' name. After outlining what he did in as much detail as he could remember, he stated: *'It is for the benefit of Mr Drewery and his suffering family that I make these facts known to you, sincerely hoping that you will make these sad truths known to some good christians in England, and that by your united energies an innocent injured man may be restored to his friends and to the sympathies of an English public. Sir I believe you will pardon the great freedom I have taken and I beg to subscribe myself, Yours, a wretched convict John Webster.'* Dated 14 June 1847, only 12 days after Thomas' ship left England.

Webster hands the letter to the Reverend G Walter and begs him to send it to the right people in England. So, as Thomas is making his way to Australia, trying to come to terms with his bleak new future, little does he know that the letter, his ticket to freedom, is on a ship travelling in the opposite direction.

Several months later, on 10 September, the *Joseph Soames* sails into Hobart, Tasmania. It is discovered that in a book at the government station *'John Webster states that a person of the name of Drewery, formerly a druggist in Hull, has been transported for seven years, charged with an offence of which he himself is guilty.'* One can only imagine how

Thomas felt when he heard the news! Thomas spends only four days in Hobart – probably in a state of shock and disbelief – before being shipped off again to Port Phillip. He arrives in Geelong on 24 September – it's his birthday. Upon arrival all the convicts are granted a Conditional Pardon. This means that Thomas is a free man but cannot leave the colony and return home. It has now been over two years since he was arrested.

Thomas remains on board a few days, then catches a steamer down to Melbourne where he enquires about work from local surgeons and druggists and manages to secure himself a position. He then writes to his wife Elizabeth telling her the good news. *'My dear, here are fresh proofs of your husband's innocence'*. He tells her about his journey and his new position. He is clearly over the moon, writing *'liberty, sweet liberty'*. He describes his life in Melbourne and the opportunities available. He sounds so enthusiastic about life in Australia and writes *'The only compensation I ask is, that government will send you and my dear children out to me respectably, not as the wife of a convict, but as one whose husband has been shamefully used. I have no wish to return yet – I can do better here.'* He asks Elizabeth to tell the press so that his innocence can be proclaimed in the newspapers, which she does.

When John Webster's letter arrives in England, Sidebottom requests an interview with Sir George Grey at the Home Office. After reading the letter and the affidavits from the new witnesses the Home Secretary agrees to investigate the case. He looks into the character and station of the four new witnesses, Webster's description of the events, particularly his description of the horse. He found the witnesses to be reliable and the description from Webster to be mostly spot on. It was concluded that the two witnesses who had sworn it was Thomas must have made a mistake. Sir George Grey issued the free pardon that very day and had it dispatched to Van Diemen's Land on the very next vessel.

There was still the question of compensation though. The Drewery family had no money. Thomas couldn't afford to pay for passage back to England and his wife certainly didn't have the money to take her and their children to join him. At the time Thomas had written to his wife saying he preferred her and the children to come to him and live in Australia, he had not known for certain that he could leave the country. So a letter from Elizabeth was written asking him what he wanted her to do and it was sent to him along with the pardon.

In the meantime, the whole story was still being told in the local newspapers. People felt so sorry for the Drewerys that money continued pouring in for Thomas and his family. Even the Chaplain, Joseph Kingsmill of the Pentonville Prison, who had met Thomas during his time there, said he wanted to contribute to the fund to give Thomas a new start. By 28 January 1848, the newspaper reported that they had already raised £50 (a year's salary). Quite a sum of money for those times. Banks and newspapers all played a role in collecting the money.

When the news finally arrived that confirmed Thomas wanted his wife and children to join him in Australia, Elizabeth wasted no more time. She packed up their home and belongings and Monday 22 May, 1848 Elizabeth and her children set sail from London on the ship *Royal*. The government paid for their passage, bedding and clothing etc. and of course she had the money that the public had raised. She was finally going to see her husband, and the children their father, after over three years!

Convict Pirates of Moreton Bay

It was a warm summer evening in December 1831. The young Captain Browning lay peacefully sleeping in his hot, stuffy, cabin on board the *Caledonia* when he was awoken by the rapid striking of the alarm bell. It was around half past three in the morning and he struggled to rouse himself from his deep sleep. As the watch-keeper on deck continued to frantically ring the bell, the signal that a boat had been spotted approaching them, the captain groped around for his clothes. He was still groggy with sleep when the door to his cabin was suddenly thrust open, and a pistol levelled at his face.

Captain Browning slowly raised his hands in surrender. The men standing before him lunged at him, seizing his arms, and roughly shoved him through the cabin door and out on deck where to his horror he discovered that the boat had been taken over by 11 armed convict men. Most of the convicts were brandishing either a musket, a pistol, or a cutlass.

The ringleader was a man by the name of William Evans. Unlike the other convicts, Evans had travelled to Sydney Cove as a free man. He had been working as a seaman on board the *Australia* but was arrested after stealing money off Captain Sleight and sentenced to seven years. He had been transported to Moreton Bay Penal Settlement to serve out his time. Evans was four years into his sentence when he saw an opportunity to escape his hellish situation and seized it.

The settlement at Moreton Bay had a terrible reputation, especially under the command of Patrick Logan. Logan was said to be a cruel man who administered brutal punishments to the convicts. Life in this penal settlement was captured in verse known as *'Moreton Bay'* which was sung by the convicts upon the death of Logan in 1830. The third verse goes:

'For three long years I was beastly treated, heavy irons on my legs I wore,

My back from flogging it was lacerated, and often painted with crimson gore,

And many a lad from downright starvation lies mouldering humbly beneath the clay,

Where Captain Logan he had us mangled on his triangles at Moreton Bay.'

It wasn't hard for Evans to convince 10 other convicts to join him in a daring escape. The night before they had taken over the *Caledonia*, they had tunnelled their way through the sandy ground into the Pilot's log hut. One by one, they quietly slipped into the Pilot's bedroom while he and a convict servant lay sleeping. In the other room four soldiers were also fast asleep. Avoiding the room with the soldiers, the convicts crept around, stripping the hut of its weapons, and managed to leave with two muskets, three pistols and two cutlasses.

Taking the ship the following night had been easier than expected. All but one of the crew were fast asleep in their hammocks at the time. The watchkeeper hadn't even noticed them until it was too late. He had sounded the alarm, but the convicts had scaled the side of the ship and jumped on deck before the crew could be mustered.

With the captain and all the crew rounded up, Evans

demanded they produce all weapons on board, which consisted of two muskets and two pistols. After surrendering their weapons, the captain was questioned about his navigation skills. Browning tried to downplay his role as the master of the ship, but the convicts didn't believe him. He was coming with them.

The convict men began arguing amongst themselves over what to do with the crew. Some wanted them to walk the plank and face certain death but thankfully they were outvoted seven to four. The pirate convicts ushered the crew overboard into the smaller boat. Browning made several attempts to join them but was thwarted each time. The crew were told to push off and were set adrift without an oar. Left alone with the pirates, Browning now feared for his life and continued to try and escape. Evans ordered the men to tie Browning up, but he continued to try and struggle free though his attempts were futile.

Once the ship was underway and land was out of sight the convicts untied Browning and directed him to take the helm and start steering towards the Navigator Islands. Browning felt certain that the pirates would only keep him alive for as long as he was useful. His plan was to befriend them in the hope that once he had navigated them to their desired destination, they would set him free. He started by sympathising with their situation, remarking that it was only natural for men to want to flee from bondage. He feigned empathy, saying he too was far from their native country.

Days passed, and Browning felt like he was slowly gaining their trust. The pirates had ordered him to sail to Rotuma Island. Browning overheard them say that Rotuma Island had been chosen as someone had heard that English whalers regularly sailed to the islands. Their plan was to stow away in their vessels so they could get back to England.

It had now been about a week since they had left the Moreton Bay Penal Settlement. Browning could feel that tensions were brewing, and it wasn't long before the pirates began turning on each other. Browning had overheard six of the pirates plotting to rid themselves of the other five. Evans, Hastings, and Smith seemed to be the ringleaders of the larger party. Browning watched on as Evans called a convict up by the name of John McDonald and without warning shot McDonald point-blank in the head.

Mayhem erupted. Hastings whipped out his pistol and fired at a man named William Vaughan, only managing to wound him in the hand and grazing his head. The pirates chased the injured man around the ship brandishing their weapons, taunting him. Bleeding and fearing for his life, Vaughan pitifully cried out for mercy. Cornered, he made a daring leap overboard catching one of the ropes. The pirates cut the ropes and he plunged into the water and was never seen again. Browning watched on in horror as another convict by the name of Conor was forced overboard too. Browning was now reeling in shock and in no doubt that these men were absolute savages. He knew his chances of survival were next to nothing.

Nearing New Caledonia, Evans and his right-hand man Hugh Hastings broke into an argument over grog. Hastings had been transported to Australia for plotting to take over the *Havannah Packet* from his employers, arriving in 1826 on board the *Marquis of Hastings*. A known troublemaker, he was sent to Moreton Bay as a secondary punishment. The following day Browning was ordered to pull into Saint Vincent Bay in New Caledonia as they needed to refill their casks with water. Once onshore it was decided that Hastings wouldn't be re-joining them. New Caledonia had a fierce reputation of being full of natives that were known cannibals. As Browning headed back out to sea, he tried to push away thoughts of what unimaginable horrors this man would face at the hands of these cannibals. He also tried not to think of what the pirates had in store for him once he had delivered them safely to Rotuma Island.

After the pirates' murderous rampage, a powerful wind whipped around the ship. They watched as the sky clouded over and turned black. The rolling swell of the waves began to build and before they knew it, they found themselves in the eye of a fierce storm. Waves crashed down upon them, washing over the deck. Above the roar of the ocean and the claps of thunder, Browning yelled out instructions to trim the sails and batten down the hatches. He was astounded to see these brutal men turn to quivering cowards in front of his eyes. As the ship thrashed about, some of the pirates fell to their knees and begged the captain to get them out of there and deliver them safely to land. Browning was so disgusted with them, he couldn't help himself and spat out that they would '*all go to the devil together*'.

Once the storm had passed Browning lay down to rest. He was both physically and emotionally exhausted. He closed his eyes and tried to let sleep take a hold of him. Thinking he was asleep, the pirates began discussing what was to be done with him. Browning instantly stiffened, straining to hear what they were plotting. The pirates conceded that on the whole Browning was a good man, but their safety had to come first. They all agreed that once he had delivered them to their desired location the ship would be scuttled and his life would be terminated. Browning spent the rest of the night desperately trying to figure out a way to save himself.

It was evening when they began to approach their final destination. Browning had come up with a plan that might save his life. He held his breath hoping none of the pirates realised that he was sailing them straight past the island, continuing onto one of the smaller islands nearby. To his relief the natives approached their ship and boarded it. Unfortunately, Browning was closely watched by the pirates so that he couldn't impart to the chief that he was a hostage of the pirate crew. The chief gifted them two casks of water and three of his women folk for their journey to Wallis Island. Before they left though, one of the pirates, Henry Halfpenny, escaped, deciding to take his chances there than with the rest of them.

Browning was ordered to set sail again and head for Wallis Island. During their journey, three of the pirates named Watson, Hogg and Smith confided in Browning that Evans was planning to scuttle the ship at Wallis Island with him and the three women onboard. The three pirates also expressed their fear that they were going to be shot by Evans. Unbeknown to Evans and his crew, Browning managed to sail straight past Wallis Island and made for Futuna. Again, they were welcomed by the local natives who exchanged goods with them, offering the pirates pigs and fruit. Browning desperately sought an opportunity to escape but none presented itself.

On 29 February they set sail again, and shortly after, arrived in waters off Savai'i in Samoa. It was here that the pirates began tearing the *Caledonia* apart. Browning begged them to spare the vessel, but it was of no use. They attacked the ship, ripping up decking and smashing up everything with crow bars and anything else they could get their hands on until they had destroyed the ship. Browning, Watson, Hogg and Smith thought their time was up, but Evans wasn't finished with them just yet. He ordered them to help pack things on to the small boat. Browning managed to save a violin to take with them too. They watched as the ship sank into the depths of the ocean and then made their way to shore.

When they arrived, the native people were extremely welcoming, particularly when the pirates explained that they had been shipwrecked! Browning was very respectful of their culture and the chief soon took a liking to him. He was invited to join hunting parties and to attend their cultural ceremonies. To repay their kindness Browning played them his violin. As he drew the bow across the strings filling the air with a sweet sound like nothing they had ever heard before, they reacted with astonishment and extreme delight, captivated by his performance. He also taught them how to dance in the European style which they enjoyed immensely. The Samoans offered him their special root drink called Kava but Browning politely declined.

Browning was overwhelmed by their generosity, openness and warmth and wanted to tell them the real reason he was there, however, he was still being closely watched by the pirates. The day after landing, Watson, Hogg and Smith approached Browning, telling him that they were leaving with the boat and asked him if he wanted to come with them. Browning declined saying that he intended on getting on the first vessel that came by.

They had been on the island for eight days when the *Oldham* sailed into view. Browning seized his moment and took a canoe out to the vessel. He shared his story with Captain Johnson, telling him he was the master of the *Caledonia* and informed him of all that had transpired. Once

Johnson's crew were on land, they asked all the remaining pirates individually who the master had been. Evans claimed to have been the master. The chief officer then made enquiries with the natives and soon discovered what was really afoot. Evans was immediately placed in irons. By the time it was all uncovered the rest of the pirates could not be found and it was suspected that the natives were hiding them.

Captain Johnson set sail with both Browning and Evans on board. It had been difficult for Browning to say goodbye to the people who had shown him such hospitality. The Chief was particularly saddened to see him go and tried to convince him to stay. Browning promised that he would return in a few moons. The chieftain gifted him pigs, and other necessities for the trip. Once the *Oldham* pulled out into the heavy seas Evans took his opportunity and jumped overboard, preferring to drown than be brought to Sydney again.

On they sailed until the *Oldham* fell in with the American ship *Milo* and Browning was given the choice of staying with the *Oldham* or transferring to the *Milo* which was bound directly for Sydney. He chose to go with the *Milo* as he was eager to get back as soon as possible. This decision turned out to be best he ever made, as soon after he said goodbye to the *Oldham* it was captured near Wallis Island and everyone on board was murdered.

Once on board the *Milo*, Browning fell dangerously ill and there were fears that he might not make it. However, Captain West and his crew took such great care of him that he recovered. On Monday, 14 May 1832, the American ship *Milo* glided into Sydney Harbour with Captain Browning onboard. He was in a weak state but happy to be back.

The convicts who had escaped were never heard of again. Captain Browning did end up returning to the South Seas and it was rumoured he married a Fijian princess. He had a long and interesting life and died in 1887, at the age of 82, and was buried at Rookwood Cemetery, New South Wales.

Australia's First Cold Case and the Man They Couldn't Hang

∽

Joseph Samuels was only 14 years old when he was sentenced to transportation for a robbery, he committed in 1795. This wasn't his first offence. He had seen the inside of the Old Bailey court room before when he was about 12 years old. On that occasion he had been arrested for Grand Larceny. He'd been found guilty but was let off with just a warning due to his young age. He wasn't so lucky the next time. The court sentenced him to seven years. He spent most of his sentence in England, serving out his time in one of their filthy, overcrowded prisons before boarding a ship to New South Wales. However, transportation did nothing to kill Samuel's love of a five-finger discount. Within two years of being in the colony Samuels was planning his next theft. At the time, he was hanging around a gang of thieves and some very shady police officers.

At around 5 p.m. on the evening of 25 August 1803, Mary Breeze locked up her house on Back Row in Sydney, which is where Phillip Street stands today. As she left her home and wandered down the cobblestone street that backed onto bush and scrub, little did she realise that the gang of thieves Samuels belonged to were watching her closely. As soon as she was out of view they descended on her property, gathering in her back garden before breaking into her house. Heading straight to her bedroom they seized her small portable desk and fled on foot.

When Mary returned at around 8 p.m. she was alarmed

to find her back door wide open. She bravely entered the house and discovered her desk missing. The desk had all her important papers plus 50 dollars, three guineas, two pieces of gold coin, trinkets, and some copper coins. She raced across the road to alert Officer Joseph Luker who was the night watchman. Officer Luker was about mid to late thirties. He was a former convict himself. Luker's shift didn't start until midnight, but he promised he would look into it then.

Luker strongly suspected his fellow watchman Simmonds to somehow be involved. At midnight when he went on duty, he searched nearby scrubland for the desk. Before the sun had risen the next day Luker's dead body was discovered on the side of the road leading to Farm Cove – where the Royal Botanic Gardens stand today. His injuries were extensive and were published in full detail in the *Sydney Gazette* with no thought for his loved ones. They described his body as being '*shockingly mangled, and with the guard of his cutlass buried in his brain*'. The sheaf was found next to his body. He suffered 16 stab wounds and contusions, with his left ear nearly sliced in half. He was attacked with so many different weapons that the police concluded there must have been at least three men involved in the brutal murder. He'd been beaten with the stolen desk, the frame of a wheelbarrow and stabbed with his own cutlass.

Several men were suspected of the murder. Constable Isaac Simmonds and Constable William Bladders were arrested for Luker's murder, but despite both being found covered in blood, there was not enough evidence to convict either one of them. Simmonds claimed the blood on him was from a nosebleed and Bladders claimed that the blood on him was from slaughtering a pig. Another Constable named John Russell, was also questioned, and arrested for breaking and entering, but, again, there was not enough evidence to convict him. All three Constables were former convicts.

Police also questioned a notorious thief, Richard Jackson, who gave a full confession to breaking and entering Mary Breeze's house. He said the plan to rob her had been the idea of Samuels. He told the court that when they approached the house they happened upon Constable Russell and told him of their plot to steal from her property. He claimed that he asked Russell to keep watch out the front as he and Samuels went in round the back. However, after robbing the house they didn't see Russell again and told the court for that reason they had no plans to share their loot with him.

As for Samuels, his fate was sealed when a witness came forward claiming to have seen him in Mary Breeze's backyard at around 6 p.m. along with another man. So, he confessed to robbing Mary but swore that he had nothing to do with Luker's murder. The court found him guilty of theft but not of the murder and sentenced him to death. All the other suspects including Richard Jackson avoided conviction.

On Monday, 26 September, 1803 at 9.30 in the morning, the NSW Corps loaded Samuels into their horse and cart to take him to the place where he was to be executed. Travelling with him was another man who had been sentenced to death, James Hardwicke. They reached their destination to find a crowd had gathered to witness the men being executed. Hangings were often regarded as a source of entertainment for people. Constable Simmonds was forced to attend.

Both men were given time for religious instruction.

Reverend Samuel Marsden had come to commence his ministrations with Hardwicke, but Samuels was Jewish and therefore had his own religious counsel. Then Samuels was questioned again about the murder of Luker and asked if he wanted to unburden himself by making a confession before he met with God.

Samuels swore that he did not kill Luker, but told the officer that whilst being held in the same prison cell as Simmonds, Simmonds had made a confession to him. Simmonds told him that Luker had discovered him with the desk so he *'Knocked him down, and given him a topper for luck!'*. Suspicion had followed Simmonds since the crime had taken place and suddenly everyone at the execution turned to look at him. There were growing discussions amongst the crowd that Samuels was a man who was about to face God and therefore would not be lying. Any doubt that they formerly had of Simmonds' involvement with the murder was now gone – but there was still no proof and no way to convict him.

At 10 a.m. the ropes were prepared and Samuels and Hardwicke were helped back up into the cart. As the noose was secured around their necks, and the officer was about to signal for the driver of the cart to pull away, a messenger arrived with a reprieve for Hardwicke. He was immediately taken down. Samuels spent the ensuing minutes praying, probably for a reprieve to come for him, but when none came the signal was given and the cart drove out from under him. As soon as he felt his weight pull at his neck the rope snapped and he fell to the ground with a thud.

He remained there motionless, with his face in the dirt. Two men hoisted him up and the cart was backed up again. They helped him up onto the cart and again placed a noose around his neck. The signal was given once more, and as the cart pulled away Samuels' body was thrust downwards and when his full weight pulled on the noose the rope began to slip until Samuels' feet were grazing the ground. The crowd was stunned, and some began proclaiming that it was the work of God.

The executioner quickly fashioned a new noose. Samuels was now unconscious and was raised up to the noose with the help of some men who put him on their shoulders. They gently lowered his body so the noose could do its work, but again the rope snapped, and he fell once more to the ground. By now the crowd was in an uproar. No one could believe what they had just witnessed. Spectators cried out that the invisible hand of God had intervened, and they began calling out for Samuels' release. The provost Marshall took off on his horse in search of the Governor and he soon returned with a reprieve. The crowd rejoiced at the news as Samuels slowly regained consciousness. He appeared confused and had no recollection of what he had just been through.

Officers began testing the ropes which had failed during the execution and found all to be sound. This was further proof to the crowd of spectators that they had just witnessed the hand of God. Heightened emotions, compassion and elation spread amongst all that had attended. Samuels was eventually led away, and although he did receive a reprieve of his death sentence, he was punished for the robbery. First, he served time at Risdon Cove in Van Diemen's Land and was then transferred to Newcastle to work in the coal mines.

The murder of Constable Joseph Luker has never been solved and remains Australia's oldest cold case. He is the first Australian police officer to be killed on duty. He was buried at the Old Sydney Burial ground where the Town Hall stands today. However, his remains were relocated to Rookwood Cemetery, though there are no records of exactly where he is buried and no headstone.

A Daring Escape from the Road Gangs of Western Australia

At 3 o'clock in the morning on 10 January, 1868 the *Hougoumont* cut through the mist and quietly sailed into Fremantle, carrying with it 279 male prisoners. The 14,000-mile trip had been fairly uneventful, but for some, the 89 day voyage from Britain had been the most bleak and miserable time of their lives.

Sixty-two of the convict men on board were political prisoners from Ireland who had been caught the year before for their involvement in the Fenian movement. Down in the depths of the ship, a Fenian by the name of John Boyle O'Reilly described his experience, *'Only those who have stood within the bars, and heard the din of devils and the appalling sounds of despair, blended in a diapason that made every hatch mouth a vent of hell, can imagine the horrors of the hold of a convict ship.'*

John had originally been sentenced to death for withholding his knowledge that a mutiny was being planned. A date had even been set for his death by firearm, but his sentence was commuted to 20 years. Before he was arrested, he had worked as a reporter. John had a sunny personality and easily made friends – a very useful trait when trying to uncover a story.

As they approached the shore, the Fremantle Prison, or the Convict Establishment as it had been previously known, loomed large. The limestone building had been built using the blood, sweat and tears of convicts, and domineered the landscape and town of Fremantle. Nearly 10,000 convicts had passed through its gates since 1850. It was here that John and his fellow Fenians and convicts would be processed and assigned work.

Sometime later they were led in groups from the ship. John looked around, taking in the surrounds, and realised that the Establishment wasn't the only prison, for so too was the thick, uninviting wild bushland. But he was not to stay in Fremantle for long. He, along with other convicts from his ship were sent to Bunbury, a coastal town which lay south of Fremantle. There they were split into gangs to work on building roads through the dense bush that was just outside the town.

At Bunbury they toiled from sunrise to sunset with the searing sun beating down on them. The intense, suffocating heat was a complete contrast to their former lives in Ireland. The days were monotonous and as they performed their back-breaking work many convicts entertained ideas of ending their life. One poor soul was so desperate that he cut his left wrist hoping to put an end to his misery, but after fainting he was led away and restored back to health. Others tried to stay positive by reminding themselves that they could be completing their sentence in the over-crowded, dark, infested prison cells back in England – at least here they were outside in nature, breathing fresh air in open spaces.

John's thoughts always turned to the same thing – escaping. He knew he could not survive 20 years of this. There were only two ways to escape – through the bush or by the ocean. The bush was considered suicide, as men before him had tried and died or turned back due to starvation and thirst – that's if the native trackers didn't find you first. John put his energy into becoming a hard worker and soon caught the attention of his overseer. For his good conduct he was pulled away from the harsh work and entrusted with a new task of running errands and delivering reports to the convict depot.

It was around this time that he began confiding in the local Reverend, Father McCabe. John had almost reached his limit. He felt so desperate that he told Father McCabe that he was considering making a break for it into the bush. The Father's response was *'It is an excellent way to commit suicide. Don't think of that again. Let me think out a plan for you.'*

Months passed and John became increasingly impatient. Finally, the Father devised a plan and set it in motion. He enlisted the help of a man named Maguire and asked him to use his contacts with the New Bedford Whaling Company to stow John away on board their vessel. Three of their whaling vessels were due to arrive in February. John agreed to wait the two months until they arrived. When February was upon them Maguire approached John with good news. Captain Baker of the whaling ship *Vigilant* had agreed to smuggle him out of the colony, but he wanted John to row out of Australian waters to meet him.

On a warm summer's evening in February, John made his move. He managed to slip out and make his way to a predetermined hiding spot at the edge of the woods and holed up under a huge gum tree. There he waited until around midnight when he heard Maguire whistle the St Patrick's Day tune signalling it was time to move out and start his escape. John, Maguire and a friend of Maguire's rode their horses throughout the night until they met a boat waiting for them. John boarded the boat at daybreak and an oarsman rowed him to the southern point of Geographe Bay to wait for the passing *Vigilant*. John had brought no food or water with him. He spent the night on the shore and woke with terrible hunger pains and yearning for a drink. The day was hot, and he spent it waiting for Maguire to come back to him with food and water.

By the afternoon of the next day the white sails of the *Vigilant* could be seen in the distance so they hurriedly pushed off in their boat and rowed out to the meeting point. But John's hopes were dashed when the *Vigilant* sailed right past them. The men rowed back to shore with the confused and disheartened John. Deflated, they found a hiding spot for him nearby and promised to return in a week. In the meantime, they would approach another whaleship and see if they could get him passage onboard.

Desperate, John took a boat the next morning. His determination spurred him on and gave him the energy he needed to get out far enough for a passing whaling ship to pick him up. He rowed all day and slept in the boat that night. The next day he spotted the *Vigilant* again and frantically waved his hands about to get their attention, but alas, Captain Baker and his crew did not spot him. Frustrated and disheartened he turned his boat around and rowed back to shore. He rowed all night and into the next day and when he finally made it back to where he had started, he felt utterly exhausted and collapsed in a heap on the sandy beach.

For the following five days he spent most of his time sleeping off his epic journey. When his friends finally returned, they brought with them good news. They had arranged his safe passage with Captain Gifford on board the whaling ship *Gazelle*. John was overwhelmed with emotion and gratitude to hear that Father McCabe had given the captain £10 to ensure he was picked up and cared for on the journey.

The next morning with renewed vigour and determination, John and his friends pushed their boat off the shore, hopped in and earnestly began rowing out. They rowed till noon, when the small boat *Clarice* met them. John said a quick goodbye to his friends and stepped onto the *Clarice* which transferred him to the *Gazelle*. He turned to take one last long look at New Holland – relieved to be leaving but saddened to be leaving his friends behind.

For the next six months, the *Gazelle* chased whales. John was astonished at the kind treatment he received from the captain and everyone on board. He wrote to the newspaper the *Irishman*, '*When the Captain knew who and what I was, he installed me cabin passenger, and as he was on a six month cruise for whales, I remained on board for that time, and every day had a fresh instance of his kindness, and of the officers and all on board.*' One of the men even saved John's life when he decided to participate in a fight with a whale. John's inexperience nearly cost him his life. He was close to drowning but the third mate, named Hathaway, saved him.

The *Gazelle* made many stops along their journey and rumours spread that John was on board being aided in his escape attempt by the captain. When the vessel reached the British occupied island of Rodrigue, which lay roughly 380 miles off Mauritius, the Governor was waiting for them. He and his officers came onboard demanding that Captain Gifford hand John over. At that point the chief mate spoke up, pointing up to the stars and stripes flying from the mast he said, '*I know nothing of any 'convict' named O'Reilly, who escaped from New Holland; but I did know Mr O'Reilly, who was a political prisoner there, and he was on board this ship, but you cannot see him – he is dead.*' Not entirely convinced, the Governor had no choice but to leave the ship.

The *Gazelle* pressed on. They had intended to stop at Mauritius but the captain did not want to risk John's capture by the English. When they reached the waters off the Cape of Good Hope the Captain accompanied John in a small boat and together they rowed out to another vessel called the *Sapphire*. The *Sapphire* was under the charge of Captain E J Seiders. Captain Gifford explained John's situation and asked Seiders if he would take him the rest of the way to New York. John said goodbye to Captain Gifford and thanked him profusely for all that he and his crew had done for him. Not only had they given him passage and saved him in Rodrigue Island, but they had also taken up a collection of money to help him on the next leg of his journey. John was overwhelmed by their generosity and made a promise to himself to repay them someday.

True to his word Captain Seiders delivered him safely to the shores of New York. Before parting he looked John square in the eyes and *'shook hands warmly with the "felon", and said he wished he could save a dozen of O'Reilly's countrymen.'* Captain Seiders handed him more money from himself and the chief mate of the *Sapphire* before sailing away.

John was so moved by all the compassion and help he had received on his journey. He was never recaptured and soon became an American citizen. He established himself in Boston, working first as a journalist then eventually becoming a part-owner of the *Pilot* newspaper. John never forgot the kindness he was shown and strove to repay all who had helped him. He wrote to several newspapers, acknowledging the men who had assisted him. He had written to the *Irishman* imploring, *'should anything happen to me, the gentlemen who assisted me shall not lose his money.'*

The years passed but John just couldn't shake off the thought of the Fenian friends that he'd left behind doing hard labour back on the road gangs in New Holland. In 1875 he, along with the help of some others, devised a cunning plan to rescue their friends ...

The Audacious Plot to Rescue Six Irish Convicts from Prison

It was 1874 when John Devoy, a former leader of the Irish Republican Brotherhood, known as the Fenians, received a letter from a convict in New Holland. It was from a fellow Fenian named James Wilson who implored Devoy to save him and the other men serving hard labour in the colonies for conspiring to liberate Ireland. His desperate plea began, *'Dear Friend, remember this is a voice from the tomb. For is not this a living tomb? In the tomb it is only a man's body that is good for worms, but in the living tomb the canker worm of care enters the very soul ... We ask you to aid us with your tongue and pen, with your brain and intellect, with your ability and influence, and God will bless your efforts, and we will repay you with all the gratitude of our natures ... our faith in you is unbound. We think if you forsake us, then we are friendless indeed.'*

Moved by his impassioned plea, Devoy took the letter to his good friend John Boyle O'Reilly. And so, the two began a cunning plot to rescue six convicts from their exile on the other side of the world. It would take two years of meticulous planning before they were ready to execute the most audacious prison break Australia had ever seen.

The six convicts were Thomas Darragh, Martin Hogan, Michael Harrington, Thomas Hassett, Robert Cranston and of course James Wilson. All were Irish rebels that had been arrested and charged with conspiring to overthrow British rule in Ireland. They had been captured and sentenced in 1867 and spent time in some of England's worst prisons before being shipped to New Holland, arriving 10 January 1868. The ship was the *Hougoumont*, and it was to be the last vessel to bring convicts to New Holland. There were 62 Fenian political prisoners in total who arrived as convicts that day. Since then, most of the Fenians had received pardons – all except these six men.

Despite their desperation to escape, their behaviour up until that point had been exceptional. They hadn't given authorities any cause to suspect what was afoot. For years they had toiled away day by day and many had been given great freedoms in their movements and work placements due to their good conduct. Leading up to the escape the only ones working inside Fremantle prison were Cranston and Hassett who were assigned as constables. They could come and go without the usual pass. Wilson and Harrington were working down at the Sea Jetty, Hogan was painting the Comptroller's house and Darragh was in and out of the prison working as a messenger.

Easter Monday was marked as the day of the great Regatta. Perth would be alive with activity for the event. People from all over Western Australia would visit to watch and take part in the festivities. There was to be all sorts of races – the Amateur Dinghy pulling race, two-oared gig race, 1st class yacht race, canoe paddling race, dinghy pulling race and much more. Perth would be buzzing with such a hive of activity that no one would notice six convicts quietly slipping out of the colony – or that was the plan.

At about 8 a.m. of the morning of the Regatta, Cranston left the prison and strolled down to the jetty where Wilson and Harrington were working. They had been assigned to quarrying and dressing stone for the new dock. Cranston confidently strolled up to the work party, swinging a key around and around on his finger. He boldly approached

Booler the warder and informed him that Wilson and Harrington were needed to assist in the removal of some furniture from Government House. Cranston reassured him that it shouldn't take long. Booler hesitated at first but seeing that Cranston had the key he agreed to let them go.

The rest of the convicts had no problem slipping away from their work assignments and were soon picked up by carriages. The carriages had been hired by four men going under the names Collins, Jones, Johnson and Taylor who had all sailed to New Holland separately. Collins had arrived five months beforehand to make preparations for the escape. His real name was Breslin, and he was in charge of orchestrating the land operations of the plot. Later Jones arrived and stayed in a separate hotel in Fremantle. The two men were only seen a few times in each other's company, not enough to raise any suspicions. Closer to the date of the escape the other two gentlemen arrived. Breslin had hired a buggy and two horses. Jones borrowed a saddle horse and one of the other men hired a horse and a two wheeled trap. Each man had his set tasks to carry out before the due date. Every little detail had been thought of and on the day of the escape the men had artfully collected arms, ammunition, clothing for the prisoners, horses, saddles, carriages, and everything they would need to get the convicts and themselves out of the colony.

Once the six men were all safely in the carriages, they sped off at great haste towards Rockingham, a distance of 14 miles. Sometime between 9 and 10 a.m. Hogan was found missing from the Comptroller's House where he was supposed to be painting. Around the same time Cranston was discovered missing. The Superintendent of the prison had told the chief warder that Cranston was not permitted to leave the prison that day as the store's office would be closed, so when they couldn't find him within the gaol, they knew something was up. Word was quickly sent around that two Fenians were missing and before long that number had increased to six.

Reports reached the police that some carriages had been seen going at an immense speed towards Rockingham and someone recalled that an American whale ship was seen just off the coast there. This was the *Catalpa* that O'Reilly had purchased to rescue the men. He had chosen a whaling ship so that it wouldn't arouse suspicion, as whaling ships were often seen along the coast of Australia. He himself, had escaped Australia in a similar vessel. Most of the crew that they had hired to make the rescue attempt were not aware of their real mission. The captain, however, knew of the plan and had helped select the vessel, equip it and organised the stowing. There was only one Irishman on board who was part of the scheme and that was Dennis Duggan. He was listed as the ship's carpenter to disguise their mission.

As they neared Rockingham, they passed a proprietor named Mr Somers who was casually standing in the entrance of his hotel. As the men drove towards him, he shouted out *'What time will the Georgette be at the timber jetty?'*. The blood drained from Breslin's face, and he responded, *'Is the Georgette coming here?'*. Mr Somers shouted back *'Yes. She's due now.'* The *Georgette* was a large steamer that could cause potential problems for them. Breslin pushed the horses into a gallop, and they raced towards their destination.

Captain Anthony had come to shore on a whaleboat with the crew and was anxiously waiting for them. The crew were still unaware of what was afoot. The crew watched Captain Anthony as he paced back and forth, back and forth, wringing his hands and furtively looking about. They knew the captain had been acting strangely and there was talk amongst them that perhaps he was planning to smuggle illegal goods. Finally, he gave the order to push the boat back out onto the water and told them not to be afraid. The crew looked at each other in alarm.

At half past 10 the prisoners finally made it to the beach. The crew watched as the prisoners jumped from the traps, grabbing their weapons, and ran towards them. In their haste to reach the boat, the wind blew open their coats to reveal prison garb. The crew were shocked into silence, believing they were about to be attacked. They immediately grabbed anything they could use as a weapon and held them up high to show that they wouldn't be overcome easily. Then the captain barked the order to stand down. Confused the crew lowered their weapons.

As soon as the prisoners were onboard the crew began to row to the sound of the captain spurring them on with urgent cries of *'Pull as if you were pulling a whale'*. The prisoners sunk down as far as they could to the bottom of the boat. They weren't even half a mile from shore when they saw eight mounted police officers reach the beach.

They pressed on and at 5 p.m. just as they were reaching a dangerous reef, the winds picked up. The sky turned an angry grey colour and ocean swell pushed their little boat about violently. Water crashed over them soaking them to the bone and they feared that the boat would become swamped. Every time the boat rose upon the crest of a wave, they could see the *Catalpa* still miles away. Suddenly there was a terrible sound – it was the mast snapping off and crashing into the ocean. Luckily the crew's quick thinking and action saved them from capsizing. As the thunderous waves kept crashing over them the crew bailed as much water as they could to save them from becoming waterlogged.

Exhausted and with no break coming in the weather they tried to hold their position. By now the prisoners were extremely sick and one broke the men's silence by asking *'Captain, do you think we will float through the night'*. Captain Anthony replied, *'Oh yes, I've been out on many a worse night'*. However, the captain had serious fears for their lives. He toyed with the idea of trying to land at Garden Island but pushed it out of his mind as he knew it would mean certain capture. So, he tried to fashion a mast using one of the oars.

It was now pitch black and the men could barely see one another. They were extremely tired, hungry and thirsty and all their provisions had washed overboard. Just as they had thought all hope was lost and that they only had minutes until the little boat would be swamped, the weather turned. The fierce gales suddenly subsided and the waves began to ease. As the sun rose, their confidence and determination returned to them and they began rowing again.

They settled into a comfortable rhythm. That was until they spotted the *Georgette* sailing straight towards them. The captain immediately took down the makeshift mast, the men dragged their oars inside the boat, and everyone lay down. They were hoping that the *Georgette* would think their boat was just a log and sail straight past them. The plan worked and the *Georgette* sailed towards the *Catalpa*. The men worried that the *Georgette* might linger there, making it impossible for them to get any closer. They sat waiting, bobbing up and down on the ocean for two painfully long stressful hours.

When the *Georgette* reached the *Catalpa* they enquired where their small boat was, as it was missing from the cranes. The mate informed him that the captain had gone ashore. The officer from the *Georgette* then asked if he could come on board their vessel. The mate's response was '*Not by a damned sight*'. Thinking that the small boat must have come to shore during the storm the *Georgette* turned around and headed back. The mate anxiously looked out at sea, wondering where on earth Captain Anthony and the men were.

When the coast was clear the crew started rowing again. They had been at it for two hours when they spotted a guard ship approaching. It was filled with police – at least 30 of them could be seen on deck and they were heading their way. The exhaustion the crew had felt after hours of rowing was replaced by adrenaline and they put their body and soul into rowing with all that they had. The prisoners armed themselves and levelled rifles in the direction of the guard boat. They were not going down without a fight.

When the crew onboard the *Catalpa* finally spotted them, they began sailing in their direction to close the distance between them faster. The police realised what was happening and tried to get between the two to cut the boat off. It was a suspenseful race to the ship and luckily the men were able to outrun the guard boat. As soon as they were close, Captain Anthony yelled out to the crew on the *Catalpa* '*Hoist the ensign!*'. The boat slammed into the ship and the crew scurried into action to secure it as quickly as possible. The guard boat was bearing down on them fast, they didn't have a second to lose. The prisoners couldn't wait for the boat to be hoisted up, so they started scaling the side of the ship with their rifles.

When everyone was safely on deck there was a resounding cheer from all the men. When the guard boat reached the *Catalpa* the prisoners recognised many of the officers and taunted them by farewelling them by name. The police officers knew they had been beaten and they gracefully made their departure, returning to shore. For the next hour everyone on board the *Catalpa* were riotous with exaltation. The prisoners cheered the captain and all the crew. They were free after years and years of captivity.

Captain Anthony, Breslin and the rest of the men who had spent months planning and stressing over the execution of this plot were finally able to breathe a sigh of relief. They had done it! And they'd accomplished it without a single loss of life. The captain thanked his crew and commended them on their extraordinary efforts. He then ordered the steward to *'Get up the best dinner the ship can afford,' 'We're hungry'*. The celebrations went into the night, and everyone onboard enjoyed a feast of canned chickens, lobsters, a range of fruits and boiled vegetables.

But by daybreak the *Georgette* was seen heading straight for them. As it approached, Captain Anthony could see that the *Georgette* was carrying a regiment of soldiers who were heavily armed. The *Georgette* was twice the size of the *Catalpa* and had been fitted out with big guns. The captain ordered the ensign to be raised again and told the crew and prisoners to ready themselves.

When the *Georgette* came alongside them, they fired a single shot at the bow of the *Catalpa*. Then the captain of the *Georgette* called out to them to give the prisoners up. Captain Anthony was having none of it. Captain Harvest threatened *'I'll give you fifteen minutes in which to heave to and I'll blow your masts out unless you do so. I have the means to do it'*. To which Captain Anthony replied, *'This ship is sailing under the American flag, and she is on the high seas. If you fire on me, I warn you that you are firing on the American Flag'*.

Captain Anthony then realised that his ship was drifting closer and closer to Australian waters. He instructed his crew to get to work and Captain Harvest thought they were preparing to come back to shore. So, he started turning his vessel around. When he finally realised what was happening, he followed the ship for about an hour before giving up and heading back to Australian waters. Everyone on board the *Catalpa* breathed a huge sigh of relief.

When the *Catalpa* finally reached New York City in August 1876 they were met by a very relieved Devoy and O'Reilly, who had been anxiously waiting for them for a long 16 months. The press swarmed them as they arrived, wanting to know every detail of the plot. They had been unsure of what the reaction would be, but they found the atmosphere was one of warmth and enthusiasm. The months of stress and anxiety for the mission had had its effect on the captain. He arrived having lost nearly 40 pounds and with grey hair shining through his once charcoal black hair. But he, and all the conspirators, had pulled off the most daring prison break in Australian history thus far and for a long time he was cheered wherever he went.

The Disastrous Voyage of *George III*

On a bitterly cold winter's day in December 1834 Captain William Moxey strode around the bustling ship bellowing orders to the crew, sending them in different directions to check that the cargo was stowed safely, before returning to his cabin and poring over the maps one last time. He was readying the ship to take the epic journey from Woolwich, England to Hobart, Tasmania. The ship, *George III*, was to carry 308 people to the other side of the world. In his care were 220 male convicts as well as guards, their families and crew.

The first seven weeks of the voyage had been smooth sailing thanks to his careful planning and good weather. Life on board the ship had settled into a predictable routine. As they approached the equator however, the relaxed feeling shared amongst those on board quickly turned to panic as the smell of smoke swept through the ship. Cries of 'fire' ricocheted around the ship and the crew dashed about desperately trying to put the flames out. In the days of wooden sailing ships, fire could be catastrophic, so the crew were well trained on what to do. Sailors employed methods such as pumping water into the hold, beating the flames with wet hammocks, stretching wet sails to prevent air from feeding the fire, and creating a chain of men passing buckets of water to douse the blaze.

Despite their best efforts the fire was gaining momentum, and to their horror, the flames began to lick the walls of the magazine, where barrels of gunpowder were stored. With no time to spare, two convicts by the names of

William Nelson and David Jones ran blindly through the thick clouds of smoke. Moments later they returned, dragging the barrels of gunpowder out of the burning room before collapsing on the floor, coughing and spluttering. They had acted just in the nick of time, saving everyone on board from certain death, but their hands were severely burned. The rim of the barrels were made of copper and were red hot. Their quick thinking and courageous, selfless act earnt them the instant respect of everyone on board.

The crew worked tirelessly until they managed to extinguish the flames. When the smoke had abated, Moxey walked around assessing the damage. He was alarmed to see that so much of the stored food had been lost. David Wyse, the Surgeon Superintendent, suggested they pull into Cape Town to replenish their supplies, but the captain rejected the idea. Instead, he put everyone on half rations and ordered the crew to sail on.

Life on board soon returned to its routine, however, after a few weeks something shifted. People on board became highly irritable. Convicts complained of being too tired to perform their tasks. At first Moxey put their lack of energy down to their smaller rations, but when several men presented with swollen bleeding gums, joint pain and red and blue spots spreading over their skin, he realised that scurvy had taken hold. Scurvy was a common illness on ships as it was caused by a lack of vitamin C. No one on board had had fresh fruit or vegetables for some time and they would not reach land for many weeks to come.

One by one, the convicts fell ill with the disease, many dying. It was imperative they reach their destination quickly. When the Tasmanian coast was finally sighted on 12 April 1835 at least 12 convicts had died. There were 60 people on board who were seriously ill – 50 of those were bedridden and unable to care for themselves.

As night fell, they rounded the southern bend of Tasmania. Out of desperation, Moxey decided to sail up the D'Entrecasteaux Channel instead of going around Bruny Island and risking being pushed out to sea. He had heard of the violent squalls that came down the hills between the North and South of Bruny Island but decided to risk it. The weather seemed calm, and visibility was good. They set off and took every precaution to navigate the Actaeon Reef which had been chartered in the Horsburgh's Directory. Captain John Horsburgh was a hydrographer who had mapped the seaways in the area, and he hadn't noted any further dangers past that point. Regardless, Moxey sailed through the channel slowly, with the leadsman checking the depth of the water while they proceeded. At around half past nine the leadsman raised the alarm that they were in very shallow water. Moxey immediately ordered the helm to be put hard a-port but it was too late, the ship struck a rock.

It hit ever so lightly at first, just grazing the rock, but then with the rising swell it crashed into it with such force the rudder tore off, throwing people to the floor. The tidal surge pounded the ship against the rock. The crew scrambled to their feet to release the cutter. As they worked to free it, they heard a terrible cracking sound over the roar of the ocean as the main mast slammed down. Wave after wave crashed over the deck, washing anything that wasn't tied down overboard. The crew struggled to stay upright as they attempted to free the boats. The first one to be released went down stern first and was immediately swamped.

Very carefully, the crew lowered another boat down into the rolling swell of the sea. To their relief the boat made it safely down and bobbed up and down on the choppy waves with the third mate, Field, at its head and 10 other passengers aboard who were nervously clutching the sides. Field figured they were only about 15 miles from Hobart. Realising the ship only had a matter of hours, before it was split into pieces, he decided to take the small boat to Hobart to get help. He pushed off and began rowing with all his might.

Despite his best efforts, he realised he was making very little progress. Frustrated, he stopped for a moment, then with renewed vigor changed course and headed to the shore instead. He needed to lighten the load, or he was never going to make it to Hobart in time, so he dropped four people off at Three Hut Point before heading back out. They took turns rowing through the night, using the light of the moon to guide them as they weaved their way carefully through the channel. Their excitement grew at every bend as they were expecting to see Hobart, but after several hours the reality that they were a lot further away from their destination hit them – in fact the ship had been stranded 60 miles from Hobart. They pushed on, making it to the port at around 8 p.m and fearful as to what had become of the people they had left behind.

Meanwhile, back on the sinking ship, the rest of the crew had clambered about the deck trying to release the other boat. As the ship smashed violently up against the rock the convicts' panicked screams could be heard over the pounding waves. The officers had locked them below deck fearing they would rush the boats. The water was rapidly rising in the hold, and most could not swim. There was a mad stampede to the hatchway with convicts knocking each other over in their headlong rush to escape the water that was now at their waists. They pleaded with the guards to unlock the hatchway and let them out. The officers levelled their muskets at them, threatening to shoot if they did not back away. The convicts screamed out for Surgeon Wyse's help. When he approached the opening they grabbed him through the grates and begged him to set them free. One said, *'you promised to stand by us'*, and he tried reassuring them by saying *'so I will'* and added, *'I shall remain here with you'*.

The water continued to rise and so too did their fear and panic. Desperately, the convicts groped around in the dark, searching their space for anything that might help them and came up with some saws and hammers. In their hysteria they began pummelling and bashing the hatchway trying to break themselves free. The officers fired several shots, but it did not stop them from fighting for their freedom.

It had only been minutes since the mast had crashed down but water was washing over the deck, taking the longboat with it, flinging it and the people who had climbed aboard from side to side until eventually it tipped overboard. There it violently rocked up and down with the treacherous waves, tangled in the rigging. Moxey did all he could to free it, even getting jammed at one point, but luckily was pulled into the boat before being seriously harmed. Once the longboat was free Surgeon Wyse rushed to climb aboard, not looking back at the convicts he left behind. He made no attempt to rescue the 50 convicts that were too sick to get out of their beds.

The 42 people crammed into the longboat pulled away from the ship just as the convicts managed to break free. They clawed their way up out of the hatchway onto the deck, but the damage was done. Most of the prisoners had already drowned. Many of them had met their watery graves within a few minutes of the ship striking the rock. Some were too sick and weak to react in time to save themselves. Others were trampled in the mad rush to the hatchway and drowned. The survivors precariously clutched each other on the port side, the only part of the ship still above water. Debris from the ship was washing over the deck. Helplessly they watched on as the longboat pulled further and further away leaving them stranded.

It took hours before Moxey made it to shore. He had trouble finding a safe place to drop the passengers as it was such a rocky coastline, but eventually pulled into Southport Beach. He dropped most of them as close to the beach as possible. Most could not swim and they battled to stay upright as the waves crashed into them as they made their way to shore. They stumbled out of the water and collapsed in an exhausted heap on the sand. Moxey and the remaining five men turned the longboat around and headed straight back to the sinking ship, hoping that it wasn't too late for the people that remained aboard.

Meanwhile the 100 or so people on board *George III* stood shivering, clinging to each other in the moonlight. At four in the morning the mizzen-mast jolted them out of their shocked state when it snapped off and joined the tangled mess that lay overboard. It had the effect of righting the ship a little so that more of the deck was out of the water. Thoughts of their imminent death must have run through their minds.

Two hours later they had all but given up hope of ever being rescued when someone spotted the glint of the longboat way off in the distance. As it pushed its way over the choppy waves a cheer went up from the relieved survivors which spurred Moxey and his crew on. Moxey pulled up beside the now mostly submerged ship. Tired and worn out, he assisted the women, children and invalids into the longboat first. There were many children who had travelled with the ship, including two newborns that had been born on the journey out. It was a tight squeeze but they managed to fit between 40 and 50 people on the longboat and took off again. The crew were exhausted but this time they were aided by the rising sun and the knowledge of where to go. They safely transported all on board much faster than the first time and once again turned and headed back to the sinking ship.

The sailors were bone-weary, but they pushed through with what little energy they had left to get back to the boat as quickly as possible. They knew that there were still so many lives depending on them. As they rowed back out in the direction of the wreck, they wondered what they would find. Would the ship be completely destroyed by now? As they drew closer, they couldn't believe their eyes when they saw not only *George III* in the distance, but also another vessel heading towards it.

Relief washed over them as they pulled up beside the sinking ship and saw that the Captain of the *Louisa* was busy assisting the remaining survivors onto his small schooner. By some stroke of luck, the *Louisa* happened to be passing by when they spotted the ship in distress. Soaked to the bone and shivering cold, the exhausted survivors settled themselves aboard the *Louisa* and took one last look at the wreck. The *Louisa* set sail for the sandy beach at Southport where the others had been dropped off, with the longboat being towed behind.

When they neared the long sandy beach of Southport the captain dropped anchor and ordered his crew to lower the smaller boats. He then sent them in the direction of the beach where they could see the marooned survivors, with instructions to retrieve them. However, when they reached the golden sands of the beach, they were informed that Assistant Surgeon McGregor was missing. He had wandered into the bush looking for help and hadn't been seen since. They continued to ferry the bedraggled, tired castaways from the beach to the *Louisa*, but when McGregor still hadn't showed up, they left a small party of men with provisions on the beach to stay and look for him.

The *Louisa* headed back out into the choppy seas and began picking up speed. The captain was taking them all to Hobart. It wasn't long before they spotted three small vessels heading straight for them. When they neared the boats, they learned that the three boats had been sent to rescue the people from *George III*. Two of the vessels returned to Hobart with the *Louisa* but the tiny paddle-wheel steamer *Governor Arthur* went to rescue the surgeon and the men who had been left on Southport Beach. The *Governor Arthur* had been equipped with appropriate provisions. When it reached the beach, they found all the men, including McGregor. They were shivering uncontrollably, suffering from cold and exposure. McGregor was close to death.

The *Governor Arthur* then made its way out to the wreck to check that there were no more survivors in need of rescuing. When they arrived, they were met with a sorry scene. *George III* was all but underwater. The only person visible was an elderly convict by the name of John Roberts. Roberts hadn't known how to swim so he had tied himself to a ringbolt in the surgeon's cabin. Sadly, he had drowned.

Accounts vary slightly as to the number of people who drowned that night but there were at least 133 in total – 127 of them were convicts. An inquiry was held to better understand what happened that fateful night. It was claimed that the officers shot two convicts by the names of Robert Luker and William Yates who were trying to escape. Many convicts came forward to testify that they saw the two convict men being shot. James Elliott, a convict, claimed *'I was in the hatchway several minutes before I could get up. The soldiers kept me down and threatened to fire; I heard two shots fired: the first shot killed Robert Luker, and about 3 or 4 minutes after another shot was fired, and I saw another man fall. When I was knocked down from the hatchway I fell upon the body of R. Luker'*. The officers denied it, claiming they were firing signals of distress only. The bodies of Luker and Yates were inspected for signs of shot marks or cutlass marks, but were so badly decomposed it was impossible to know for sure or even to tell if it was really them.

The personal accounts given during the inquiry varied so much no one will ever truly know what happened and why so many convicts lost their lives. The court of inquiry did find that Moxey and the officers were free of blame and that their navigating had been well done. It was just bad luck that the rock was there and had never been spotted before. That fateful rock is now known as the King George and appears on nautical charts.

The Tea Sweeteners

In a dark corner, in the dank depths of the *Phoenix* hulk John Knatchbull whispered his cunning plan to escape into the ear of Alfred Turner. Turner listened on in interest as Knatchbull described how he and some of the other convicts planned to take over a ship and sail over 7,000 nautical miles to South America. If anyone could safely navigate them through treacherous waters, it was Knatchbull. Before being transported he had spent years in the British Navy and had risen through the ranks to become a captain. He knew his way around a ship better than any man.

Knatchbull's career had ended in March 1818 when the Navy decided to downsize after Waterloo. Knatchbull retired on a full pension, but the payments he had come to rely upon abruptly stopped when the Navy discovered that he had racked up a sizeable debt in the Azores. With no money coming in Knatchbull turned to a life of crime and six years later found himself standing before a judge in the Surry Assizes. He was sentenced to 14 years transportation for stealing with force and arms. He arrived in the colony in April 1825.

Both Knatchbull and Turner had recently been charged with forgery on top of their original sentences. They had been moved temporarily to the decommissioned ship the *Phoenix*, which was permanently moored at Lavender Bay. They spent their days working from dawn to dusk carrying out tasks such as quarrying stone and cutting timber for new building projects. They were waiting to be taken to Norfolk

Island, a tiny dot of an island in the vast South Pacific Ocean more than 900 miles from Sydney.

In 1825 Norfolk Island had been resettled as a secondary punishment site and there were terrible rumours circulating amongst the prisoners that the isolated outpost was a living nightmare. These rumours were confirmed when a group of convicts were sent from Norfolk Island to Sydney to give evidence at a trial. Judge Roger Terry was shocked to see *'Their sunken glazed eyes, deadly pale faces, hollow fleshless cheeks and once manly limbs shrivelled and withered up as if by premature old age, created horror among those in court. There was not one of the six who had not undergone from time to time, a thousand lashes each and more. They looked less like human beings than the shadows of gnomes who had risen from their sepulchral abode. What man was or ever could be reclaimed under such a system as this?'*

Like all the men on board the *Phoenix*, Turner was dreading going to Norfolk Island. This was Turner's third offence. When he was only 16, Turner had stood at the bar of the Old Bailey in London. He was found guilty and imprisoned for six months for stealing shoes, clothing, linen, teaspoons and a scent bottle. At 19 years old he had been sentenced to seven years transportation for theft. At the trial Turner unsuccessfully attempted to poke holes in the accuser's testimony *'It appears to me a very strange thing that the witness states that he had plenty of time to see me pass, and I had no bundle; now, according to the evidence, there is two pairs of sheets, four pillow-cases, four towels, and some other things, and it would have taken a large handkerchief to have tied them in; and how is it possible they should be conveyed away without his seeing them? and again, she accused me of taking eighteen shillings and nine sixpences, and now states that there was but 22s. in all.'* He was roughly halfway through this sentence when he was caught with a forged bank order for payment of 10 pounds sterling. He was indicted for falsely making, forging and counterfeiting the order and found guilty.

Turner listened on in horror as Knatchbull whispered his devious plot to poison the crew and guards! With the help of a merchant friend in Sydney, Knatchbull had obtained four pounds worth of arsenic. The deadly chemical had been secretly sown into a pillow belonging to a convict named Smith, for safe keeping. They planned to smuggle the arsenic onboard the ship that would sail them to Norfolk Island. The convict assigned to cooking their meals would slip the lethal dose of arsenic into the coppers, lacing the crew and guards' pea soup. Once the toxic powder took effect, the convicts would seize the ship and Knatchbull would sail them to South America.

As much as Turner yearned to be free of his confinement, he was sickened at the thought of poisoning so many innocent men. Arsenic poisoning was a horrible way to die! He may have had a criminal past, but he was just a petty thief, not a murderer! He feigned his enthusiasm to Knatchbull and kept his concerns to himself.

The more Turner thought about the plot the more uneasy he felt. As Turner fought with his conscience, he overheard a conversation between Knatchbull and his conspirators. Turner strained to hear what the men were saying. In hushed tones the men agreed that only 12 of them would be sailing to South America. The remaining 50 odd convicts, which included Turner, would be made to walk the plank and face certain drowning. Horrified, Turner made a decision then and there to do everything in his power to thwart their plans.

Fearing for his life, Turner discretely requested an audience with the captain and informed him of the plan that was afoot. Alarmed, the captain supplied Turner with pen, ink and paper and asked him to detail the plot. It was immediately sent to Windeyer and Thomson, two magistrates of Sydney. The magistrates weren't really convinced that anyone would do such a despicable thing. They told Turner to keep quiet and alert the captain if or when it was about to take place.

A few days later the convicts shuffled their way onto the *Governor Phillip*, the ship that would take them to Norfolk Island. Turner watched on as Smith successfully smuggled his pillow with the arsenic past the unsuspecting guards. By now there were about 15 – 20 convicts in on the plot. Once they were settled aboard, the convicts were split into messes, and each group nominated a cook. David Hannan was selected as the cook who would lace the coppers with the arsenic. Before he could carry out the diabolical task of poisoning the crew and guards, he needed to pilfer a knife.

Once the sun had set and the daily tasks had been completed, the convicts passed the night by singing at the top of their lungs. Loudly they clapped their hands and stamped their feet to the beat to conceal the noise of the jagged knife sawing through their irons. It would take several days to cut through each man's irons and the chains that ran between their legs without the guards' knowledge. Turner anxiously observed them.

When Knatchbull and his conspirators were getting closer to being ready to execute the next step of their evil plot, Turner seized his chance. He borrowed a newspaper from a sergeant on duty and quickly scribbled the words *'beware of poison'* and *'look to the irons'* in the margins without any of the other convicts noticing and cautiously handed the newspaper back to him. When the sergeant read the message, he immediately sought out Captain Richards. Upon hearing that the plot was underfoot, both men took Turner into their protection and questioned him.

By now the ship lay just off Lord Howe Island, it was late in the evening, and the wind ripped through the rigging. Captain Richards ordered the Chief Officer, Mr Hindmarsh, to shorten the sails and ready himself for any eventuality. The officers were armed with dirks and firearms, and they clomped down the wooden steps and into the depths of the ship where the convicts were held. When Knatchbull saw the officers descend into their space he was ready to start a riot, but on noticing they were armed he held back. One by one, the officers went about inspecting the irons. The convicts had done such a great job of filing them that it was hard to find the place where they were cut.

Knowing that Knatchbull was the ringleader the officers quickly seized him, hauled him upstairs to the top deck and handcuffed him. He was winched up to the main-brace and left dangling mid-air, his feet kicking wildly in frustration. The officers systematically searched every convict and soon discovered the arsenic on a convict named Wright.

For the rest of the trip, security was stepped up and a close eye kept on the convicts. When they arrived at Norfolk Island, the convict men involved in the plot were marched to the gaol and confined with double irons. The planned conspiracy was reported to the commandant, Colonel Morrisett, who ordered a full and thorough investigation. All findings were sent to Sydney and handed to the Governor.

News of the attempted poisoning soon spread around Sydney and an article about the incident was published in the *Sydney Gazette*. At the time, Sydney residents were used to hearing plots of escape and criminal intent, so nothing really shocked them anymore. However, this was a sensational story that had everyone talking. This gang of poisoners were nicknamed the 'Tea Sweeteners'.

Knatchbull's name became more well-known than the famous bushrangers of the time. He was respected and looked up to by other criminals and he used this influence to hatch another plot, this time more devious and more cunning, and on a much bigger scale than his last scheme.

The First Fleeters and their Struggle for Food

The First Fleet left England on 13 May 1787 comprising 11 ships in total. Six of the ships were transporting convicts, three were fully stocked with food, supplies and equipment and two were naval ships. There were around 1,500 mouths to feed and they took with them enough food to last about two years. It was hoped that the new colony would be able to produce their own food when that supply was exhausted. Each ship was crowded with every supply that they thought would be necessary, from casks of water, tools, seeds, fishing hooks, tents, medical supplies, to pens for animals. Captain Phillip knew that there was a real urgency to sow the land immediately upon arrival, as the voyage would eat almost a year into their two-year supply of food.

When the convicts were first loaded onto the ships at Portsmouth, they were already in poor health due to their long incarceration in infested, putrid, and disease-ridden prisons. Many of the prisons had poor ventilation, no food allowance for the prisoners and no fresh water. Surgeon John White, the head physician on the First Fleet, strongly recommended that Captain Phillip allow more fresh food in the rations to overcome any existing sickness amongst the convicts.

Before the ships even left the port some convicts had died from the poor conditions of being chained together in overcrowded filthy, dank conditions below deck. The clothing of many of the female prisoners in particular was threadbare. Captain Phillip had his work cut out for him. He tried to make conditions better for the convicts by ordering the ships to be washed and smoked. He also increased their rations. Once they got sailing the general health of the prisoners improved with the sea air, though it did take some time for them to find their sea legs.

The First Fleet made several stops along the way which was an opportunity to stock up on as much fresh food and livestock as they could. When they reached Rio de Janeiro, they stayed for about a month and enjoyed fresh fruit and vegetables. When they left, they loaded the ships with as much as they could. They enjoyed an abundance of oranges. Every passenger was able to have several oranges per day. They also stocked up on seeds and plants for the new colony and an immense amount of rum – 65,000 litres of it to be exact. There was so much purchased that they had to reorganise the cargo on all the fleets to fit it on board. Unfortunately, they later discovered that the rum was of poor quality. Robert Ross was of the opinion that *'in taste and smell it is extremely offensive'*.

They experienced all kinds of weather, from suffocating, searing heat to freezing cold temperatures, not to mention the occasional heavy storms that flooded the decks. Cockroaches, rats, bed bugs and fleas overran the ships. Despite their best efforts, a number of livestock that they had picked up at the Cape of Good Hope began dying. Weevils decimated much of the wheat and barley and the seeds needed for growing crops in the new settlement rotted from the heat and were found to be useless once planted.

Up until their arrival, Port Jackson had been home to the Gadigal people, who had been harnessing the local environment for thousands of years to provide themselves with a sustainable food source. The arrival of around 1,500 hungry Europeans disrupted this delicately balanced system. The new arrivals decimated some of the wild food sources and eventually everyone was forced to branch further and further out to source food.

The different cultures had very different ideas about what constituted food. The British brought with them their beliefs on what a meal should consist of, which was in stark contrast to the Aboriginal culture. The food they ate, the way they sourced that food, the way it was cooked and served, was so very different to the Gadigal people's way and attitude. Botanist, Joseph Banks, spoke of the need for the newcomers to learn to source and eat local vegetables if they wanted to become self-sufficient.

They did experiment with wild food to supplement their rations. Drinking tea was such a comforting custom but as tea was not part of the rations it was sorely missed. They experimented with different local leaves until they discovered the Sarsaparilla leaf could be used. It tasted like liquorice and became known as 'sweet tea'.

Foraging to feed that many was just impossible. It was also quickly discovered that any animal they killed for its meat would become flyblown in the heat. Lt Ralph Clark commented on 7 February 1788 *'the Mutten which had been kild yesterday morning was full of maggots nothing will keep 24 hours in this country'*. Without some kind of refrigeration, fresh meat and fish had to be distributed and eaten immediately.

Upon arrival the convicts had quickly been set to work clearing land for sowing. However, the tools that they had brought were found not to be strong enough to hack through the hardwoods of the dense Australian bush. Clearing the land proved to be a slow process and they had started sowing late summer, which was not an ideal time of the year. The land and the weather were not like anything back home and there were few men who knew much about farming.

The spot they chose to sow the crops was named Farm Cove and was situated where the Royal Botanic Gardens stands today. Everyone, including the convicts, were given seeds to sow and were strongly encouraged to create their own patches. Garden beds dotted the surrounding areas of the settlement. Convicts were even given free time on Saturday afternoons to tend to their gardens. Despite Captain Phillip requesting the government to send convicts who were skilled in farming and building, most of them that had been transported were petty thieves from the slums of London.

The results at first were disheartening, but as they reached spring and their experience grew, so too did their crops. They found that the quality of the soil around Port Jackson was sandy and generally poor for growing the kinds of crops they needed. They also had bad luck with their livestock. Only days after their arrival they lost a handful of sheep to lightning during a heavy storm. Captain Phillip noted, *'This country is subject to very heavy storms of thunder and lightning, several trees have been set on fire and some sheep and dogs killed in the camp since we landed'.*

Within weeks of their arrival the number of sick and dying increased dramatically due to their inability to source enough local fresh food. The early signs of scurvy had appeared on the voyage but had been kept at bay, now the disease ravaged the settlement. Many suffered from dysentery too, which meant that even with fresh fruit, their bodies could not overcome scurvy. Arthur Bowes Smyth had acted as surgeon to the crew on board the *Lady Penryn*. In his journal he wrote with alarm in February that the sick were numbering *'upwards of 100 sick'* with Lieutenant Collins *'expected not to live'*. According to Bowes Smyth that number grew to 200 by March.

In the beginning, the Governor fed everyone with more food than the Navy Board recommended. Men were given roughly 3,500 calories a day. Women were given two thirds of the men's allowance. Children received one third of the men's allowance though the older children got a little bit more. Surprisingly, the convicts were given the same amount of rations as the marines and civil servants, except for one difference – the convicts did not receive a daily allowance of alcohol.

The ration consisted of flour, salted pork or beef, dried peas, butter, and rice. By today's standard the diet seems monotonous and bland, but in those days, it was standard fare. For many, having a guaranteed meal every day was a luxury. So many of them had been living on the streets of London not knowing when or where their next meal was coming from. Early maps show communal cooking areas within the settlement. With the flour they could make bread, baking it themselves like damper or at the bakehouse that was situated on the waterline of the western side, near where Cadman's Cottage is today. Flour could also be used to make dumplings or puddings for their stews or to thicken it up. Rice could be used to make a type of gruel or to make stews go further.

It took weeks for all the stores to be unloaded from the ships. At first they were just placed on the ground and covered up, but this attracted insects. Makeshift storehouses were quickly erected for better safe keeping, but it would be months before a proper storehouse could be built. As their stores of food plummeted, the number of thefts for food rose. It got to the point were Captain Phillip had no choice but to introduce severe punishments for anyone caught stealing food. In February 1788 four men – Barrett, Lovell, Hall, and Ryan were caught stealing beef and pease from the stores. Ryan was sentenced to 300 lashes, but the other three convicts were sentenced to death. On the 27 February, the day of their execution, Lovell and Hall were reprieved and banished but Thomas Barrett was hanged from a tree between the male and female convict camps.

On 13 March Phillip introduced the first food rationing. Food rationing was a weekly event, but it was discovered that convicts weren't able to plan their food out for the week. Many consumed it all in a matter of days and were left hungry for the remainder of the week. Some people were thieving and gambling away their rations, so authorities began handing out the rations twice a week instead. Food became a way of keeping the convicts in check as they had to muster twice a week to receive it and had to work hard for it. Later, when the situation became very serious the administration began handing out the ration daily.

In October 1788, the *Sirius* was sent to the Cape of Good Hope to get them more food and seeds. It was about an eight-month round trip. They returned in May 1789 with much needed supplies but only enough to keep them going for a short while. By this time though they had begun cultivation in the Parramatta area where they had discovered richer soils. They continued to grow at Farm Cove too and were able to show a harvest of potatoes, cabbages, turnips and the like, though the amount of locally harvested food was very small. To prevent thieving, they had also started to grow crops on Garden Island.

The food crisis was a constant worry. Watkin Tench wrote *'Famine ... was approaching with gigantic strides, and the gloom and dejection overspread every countenance.'* It had now been nearly two years since they had left England. Captain Phillip had asked the authorities to send more supplies but, so far, none had been forthcoming. The feelings of desperation and isolation grew. Tench described *'every morning from daylight until sun sunk, did we sweep the horizon in hope of seeing a sail.'* Their only choice was to cut the rations even further.

Little did they know that back in England the *Guardian* was readying to set sail with almost a thousand tonnes of supplies to aid the colony. They had vegetables, grain, herbs, fruit, and a variety of livestock, as well as men with agricultural skills and qualified convict tradesmen. Sadly, when the *Guardian* was only a few weeks away from arriving in the colony it hit an iceberg and the voyage was abandoned.

Desperate, Captain Phillip sent the last two ships in the colony – the *Sirius* and *Supply* – to Norfolk Island carrying hundreds of convicts and marines. He had recently received news that the harvest at Norfolk Island had been successful, so he thought sending some people there would alleviate some of the pressure off the settlement in Sydney. Once they had unloaded the convicts and their stores the *Sirius* would travel to China to pick up emergency provisions. Unfortunately, after they unloaded the passengers, the ship ran aground and was wrecked. This was a devastating blow to the colonists. The loss of the *Sirius* meant that they only had one ship left. The small ship, the *Supply,* was their only hope of getting to a foreign port to seek assistance. When the news of the wreck reached Sydney, Captain Phillip cut the already halved rations even further. Nervously, he sent their last ship to Batavia for supplies. The colony was now completely alone, and everyone felt it acutely.

By now the salted food that had come with them was so

old it shrank when cooked. Watkin Tench noted *'We soon left off boiling the pork as it had become so old and dry that it shrunk one half in its dimensions'*. Work hours were reduced and the little work they could find the energy to do was solely focussed on obtaining wild and cultivated food to supplement their rations. Tench also noted *'The insufficiency of our ration soon diminished our execution of labour. Both soldiers and convicts pleaded such loss of strength as to find themselves unable to perform their accustomed tasks. The hours of public work were accordingly shortened or, rather, every man was ordered to do as much as his strength would permit'*.

Relief finally came on the afternoon of 3 June 1790 when the first ship of the Second Fleet was spotted sailing into the harbour. The colony erupted in excitement at the sight of the *Lady Juliana*. People cheered and hugged each other. The *Lady Juliana* not only brought with her much needed food but also the first letters from home. Tench reported *'"Letters, letters!" was the cry. They were produced and torn open in trembling agitation.'* It also brought the news of the *Guardian,* which did not surprise Captain Phillip who had long suspected that something of that nature had occurred.

Weeks later the rest of the Second Fleet arrived in a pitiful state, but it was able to greatly alleviate the food shortages and avoid what would have been certain death for the First Fleeters.

The Sinking of the *Guardian*

∼

When word reached England in early 1789 that the fledgling colony of New South Wales was in dire need of food and supplies, that their very lives were dependent on England's help, King George III immediately authorised a ship to be urgently dispatched. *HMS Guardian*, which was only five years old, was selected to make the journey. Lieutenant Edward Riou was assigned as the commander of the ship. He was only 27 years of age when appointed but he had years of experience, including as a midshipman to Captain Cook's third voyage of discovery in 1776. Riou had actually joined the navy at the tender age of 14 and had served in the French Revolutionary Wars.

It took months to organise and load the ship. Firstly, they had to convert it so she could hold as much cargo as possible. At 140 ft long she was bigger than any ship of the First Fleet and once converted she was able to carry 900 tons of cargo. Botanist Joseph Banks had written to King George III recommending that a shed be built on its deck to accommodate plants and trees that could not be easily propagated by seed. He also suggested that two gardeners travel with the ship to take good care of all plants. The King considered his proposal and approved it, so a shed was built on the top deck.

When Governor Phillip had written from Sydney Cove in 1788 begging for more supplies he had carefully thought about the colony's needs and set out what was required. He could only hope that his letter was received well and that it was acted upon swiftly. Since sending the letter, the situation in the colony had grown wretched. They were on the brink of starvation and Phillip had had no choice but to continually cut their rations. In his letter he requested more food, clothing, tools, medicine, implements for agriculture, as well as overseers who could keep the convicts in line as the marine officers refused to do so. In addition, he spoke of their need to have convicts that had skills to further develop the colony.

Every request that Phillip made was met tenfold. The *Guardian* was loaded up like no other ship that had gone before her. Every available space was used to transport plants, trees, cloth, clothing, lumber, grain, herbs, and fruit. They took 93 pots containing vegetables and a collection of the healthiest livestock including sheep, cows, horses, goats, a few deer, rabbits and poultry. The *Jackson Oxford Journal* remarked in May 1790 that *'Her deck was a complete garden'*. Phillip also had his wish of skilled convicts met. Of the 25 convicts that were chosen there were butchers, carpenters, and blacksmiths. The overseers were also highly skilled. James Smith & George Austin had previously been employed as gardeners in the King's Botanic Gardens at Kew and most of the other overseers that were sent had experience in farming, with one being a surveyor and an engineer.

On 12 September 1789 they were finally ready to set sail. They had originally intended to leave Portsmouth at the end of June but had soon discovered that they needed more time. In fact, another ship bound for Sydney Cove, the *Lady Juliana* left one month before them with over 200 female convicts on board. The *Guardian* was a fast ship and able to sail a more direct route down the African coast and overtake the *Lady Juliana*.

They had had a relatively good run when they pulled

into the Cape of Good Hope. Captain Riou was alarmed to hear that John Hunter had visited the port earlier in the year from Sydney Cove to buy more needed food. Word was that the colony was in even bigger trouble than they thought, and this spurred Captain Riou into loading up the ship with more provisions and making a hasty exit so they could relieve their hungry friends in Sydney. He bought more cattle, horses and 150 fruit trees, sailing out on 11 December.

It was two days before Christmas when through the thick rolling fog Captain Riou spotted a huge body of ice about twice the size of the main mast almost upon them. They were making really good time. Riou noted in his journal *'The horizon became clouded all around and in less than a quarter of an hour we were again shut up in a thick, close general mist and scarce able to see the ship's length before us. From this it was apprehended there were many more such islands of ice floating in these seas, which appeared very dangerous'.*

The following day the captain commanded his officers to lower some of the small boats they had onboard and go and collect large lumps of ice that were floating near the large island of ice. They had such a high demand for water due to so many passengers on board, not to mention all the animals and plants that needed to be watered regularly. The officers rowed out towards the great island of ice, careful not to get too close, and began collecting large blocks that bobbed up and down in the water surrounding it. Their attention was focussed on the water, so they didn't see a huge piece of the ice break off the highest point of the island and were startled when it came crashing down into the sea right near them. They soon had all the ice they could collect and headed back to the ship. Once on board, the thick fog returned, wrapping itself around them so they could barely see the water slapping against the ship.

All of a sudden, the entire ship shuddered and vibrated and there was an almighty crashing sound like thunder. The passengers scrambled to clutch whatever part of the ship they could in an effort to try and stay upright. The ship bashed repeatedly against the island of ice that projected further under water than they realised, and the crew sprang into action scrambling to inspect the damage. The passengers were still holding on for dear life and they held their breath, hoping that it was over, but with one last terrifying tug they felt the rudder being ripped away, heard the tiller break into pieces and, like a rubber band being snapped, they were set adrift.

Down in the hold the crew were confronted with six feet of water. For the next 24 hours they worked tirelessly without pause trying to get on top of their dire situation. They patched the hole with sail cloth and straw and pumped the water out of the hold. When they had the water level down to two feet, they allowed themselves a break. They felt triumphant that they had overcome the worst, until their quick fix pulled apart and within no time at all the ship had filled to 10 feet. Every able body on board, including the convicts, threw themselves into pumping the water out. In their desperation to lighten the ship, they decided to commit to the deep all the cows, horses, sheep and other livestock as well as their fodder. The great lumber they had stored on board had to go as well as the guns and the beautiful garden. The heavy items that they had picked up at the Cape of Good Hope such as bags of wheat, flour, barley and pease were all thrown overboard – anything to help lighten their load.

At half past nine in the evening one of the chain pumps

broke. The wind had picked up and waves crashed over the decks. The captain ordered some of the men to shut and cover the hatchways with tarpaulin to try and keep more water from getting into the hold of the ship. As the men began to really tire the captain split them into two watches so they could grab some rest alternately. He handed out refreshments consisting of biscuits and cheese and a dram of rum. He was very careful not to give them too much alcohol. Just enough to give them some energy to keep going. Every hand was needed to help. Philip Schaeffer, who was onboard with his ten-year-old daughter Elizabeth, described *'My poor child had to stand all night in water, and had to serve the men with liquor when they rested from the pumps and do other work as well.'*

By the time the sun rose on the morning of Christmas Day everybody on board was utterly spent, their clothes were saturated, and they had not gained any advantage on the increasing water leak. The wind had badly damaged the masts during the night and the ship continued to be beaten by waves. Ominous black clouds were forming overhead. The captain had severely injured his hand by trying to move a heavy cask. Feeling defeated, he gave the order to hoist the smaller boats over the side of the ship and prepare for debarkation.

As the crew launched the boats, Captain Riou retreated to his cabin and began writing a letter to the Secretary of the Admiralty. Riou had decided to stay with the sinking ship. Once he had completed writing the letter he sealed it and handed it to Mr Clements, the master, then he addressed his crew, telling them *'that he was determined to continue on board, in the discharge of his duty; but if they thought their lives would be more safe by trusting to their boats, than by remaining with him, they were at full liberty to go, and he would bear testimony to their good conduct'*. Of all the 123 people on board 62 decided to remain or were unable to get on a boat. Amongst the people who decided to go were one third of the ship's crew.

After parting ways with the *Guardian*, and everyone who remained on board, the people on the four little boats tried to stick together and make their way back to land. The captain had put aside provisions for each boat such as masts, sails, food, water, and a compass. But they had so much trouble launching the boats with the tremendous waves crashing down upon them that they struggled to lower the provisions into them. One of the jolly boats had no provisions at all. The boats tried to get alongside each other and managed to share some of their provisions, but one boat in particular had very little for all the people they had on board.

As the little boats were flung around in the tremendous swell Clements watched as one boat sunk and another disappeared from view. The remaining two boats tried to stick together and make their way north, but it proved impossible, and they were driven apart. Days passed and the remaining 15 survivors huddled up to one another to try and keep warm in freezing conditions in their open boat. There was no escaping the wind and they were constantly splashed by the icy cold sea water.

Within days of leaving the wreck they realised they were running out of water fast. They tried rationing, using the bottom of a tobacco canister to measure out each portion. They endeavoured to survive on roughly a quarter of a litre for each person per day. After four days their food was running low too. On day five Clement said *'many people this day drank their urine'*. Many stopped eating as they could not swallow without some moisture in their mouths. Out of desperation some succumbed to drinking sea water. But the sea water didn't rehydrate them; it made it so much worse and would have caused delirium, hallucinations, and vomiting. And then on day nine, with some being on the verge of death, the gunner spotted a ship in the distance. Clement said, *'Our joy at this sight was great beyond expression'*.

The French ship, the *Viscountess of Brittany* picked them up and sailed them back to Table Bay. The journey took 15 days and when asked about the fate of the *Guardian* they assumed it had sunk and all on board had perished and the sad news was sent back to London. When they had left the *Guardian,* it was roughly 400 leagues from the Cape of Good Hope which is about 1,380 miles.

Meanwhile, the men on board the *Guardian* spurred into action. They had no ability to steer without their rudder and they could not keep the leaking at bay. They were wrapped in a blanket of fog and rain and sometimes hail came down upon them. Their situation was extremely bleak, but everyone on board was determined to keep trying to stay afloat – their lives depended on it. The men continued fighting against the ensuing water leak but were utterly exhausted. They worked around the clock. Some used strung up sail cloth to make beds on part of the quarter deck so that they could grab snippets of sleep where they could. With whatever strength they could muster they threw themselves into the hopeless battle against the rising water. The ship was going to sink, they knew this was a certainty. It was just a question of when and if they could reach land or find help before that happened.

They laboured on for days and must have felt their hope fading when a Dutch packet-boat was spotted heading towards them. They had been discovered just in the nick of time. Packet boats were medium in size and had been designed for delivering mail. They sailed through the water at greater speed and looked quite different to other boats. They travelled on fixed routes and carried important mail, despatches, money, and financial documents. The packet-boat had come from the Spice Islands and Batavia and fell in beside the sinking ship, helping guide it through the treacherous waters back to the Cape of Good Hope.

When they arrived at the Cape of Good Hope, they looked a sorry sight as they staggered into the colony extremely weary. Most were very ill, with swollen legs and scantily clad. The *Guardian* was well beyond repair and after one fierce gale it was ripped away from its moorings and washed up on the beach. When news reached England that the *Guardian* had arrived at the Cape there was much surprise and rejoicing.

Over the next few months, first the *Lady Juliana*, followed by the ships of the Second Fleet, arrived in the Cape. Captain Riou gave them what little supplies he had left to send to Sydney. Most of the provisions had been thrown overboard and a lot of what was left was '*perfectly spoilt and useless*' according to Captain Riou. The convicts were sent with the Second Fleet. Captain Riou actually wrote to Secretary Stephens commending the efforts of the convicts and petitioned their freedom and thanks to his letter the British Government awarded the 20 convicts pardons on the condition that they were not to return to England before their sentence had expired. Tragically, the three other little boats were never seen again.

The Extraordinary Story of Mary Bryant – First Fleeter, Wife and Mother

∽

As the sun rose up over Sydney Cove on the morning of 29 March 1791, a rumour was spreading around the small colony like wildfire. Convicts had escaped with a boat! The news whipped around them, and they stopped what they were doing to speculate - who was missing? How did they manage to steal the government's boat and where will they go? It was soon discovered that Mary Bryant, her husband and her two small children, along with six other convicts, had made their escape during the night.

Mary was born in the bustling village of Fowey in South Cornwall in 1765. Fowey was a maze of narrow streets that led to the steep bank of the river estuary. Her father worked as a mariner on the twisting waterways that joined the picturesque towns. Fowey had once been an important trading centre, but since the trade had begun favouring Plymouth the fortunes of the harbour were in decline. Life for the Broad family must have been a struggle.

Mary was 5 feet 4 inches tall with long brown hair and captivating grey eyes. She was only 21 years old when she was arrested and charged, along with two other young women, with robbing a woman by the name of Agnes Lakeman of her silk bonnet and her goods – probably her jewellery. In the docks at the assizes in Exeter the three female offenders received the shocking news that they were to be hanged for their crimes. This sentence was later commuted to transportation beyond the seas for a period of seven years. Mary was held in an Exeter prison until she was transferred to a prison hulk in Plymouth called the *Dunkirk*.

Her time on the *Dunkirk* was horrid. The weather had been unmercifully extreme with constant storms and heavy rainfall which made its way down to the dark depths of the ship where the convicts were held. Everything was damp and musty. The *Dunkirk* had a reputation of being a brutal place for women. The marines were said to have abused their power with the women on board, which resulted in a Code of Orders being drawn up in a futile attempt to make life better for the women and offer them a morsel of protection. It was during her incarceration here that Mary discovered that she was with child.

It would be a year from the date she was arrested to when she was finally moved to the transport ship the *Charlotte* that would carry her and roughly 88 male convicts, about 19 other female convicts, 45 marines and approximately 24 crew to New South Wales. This was just one of the 11 ships of the First Fleet that were set to make the biggest migration to date. *Charlotte* was 105 feet long and 28 feet wide and was a two-decked, three-masted barque, with a very comfortable height of six feet and six inches between decks.

Amongst the convicts transferred from the *Dunkirk* to the *Charlotte* was William Bryant who had been convicted at Launceston Assizes in 1784. Like Mary he had been sentenced to death, but his sentence was later commuted to seven years. William was in his late twenties and had spunk and a boldness that often got him into trouble. He had been arrested for impersonating two of Her Majesty's seaman and receiving part of their wages. Before his arrest he had been working as a fisherman and mariner just like Mary's father had been. The two of them quickly struck up a friendship.

The *Charlotte* left Portsmouth, England along with the 10 other ships of the First Fleet in May 1787. William and the rest of the men were shackled with heavy leg irons. As the months passed Mary's belly grew until she gave birth on the ship. Surgeon-General, John White noted in his journal *'Mary Broad, a convict, was delivered of a fine girl.'* Mary named her daughter Charlotte after the ship.

Once the First Fleet arrived and settled in the new colony, Mary and William were married just four days after landing. They were given a hut and William's fishing skills were put to good use. His contribution to the colony's food supply was invaluable and he was able to negotiate the privilege of keeping part of his catch of fish for himself. Despite this indulgence, within a year of their arrival William was caught selling part of the fish meant for the government stores and received 100 lashes. He was allowed to keep working as a fisherman as the colony desperately needed his skills, but a very close eye was kept on him.

In April 1790, Mary and William welcomed the birth of their child Emanuel into their family. By this time the colony was on the brink of starvation. The ration had been drastically reduced and the food that they did receive was pitiful. Tench noted *'The pork had been salted between three and four years, and every grain of rice was a moving body, from the inhabitants lodged within it.'* Relief came with the arrival of the Second Fleet but there was still doubt over whether the colony would be able to sustain itself. It was around this time that William and Mary hatched a plan to escape the colony and what they deemed a certain death. They could not watch their children starve to death.

Over the coming months Mary and William set about carefully collecting provisions. They knew they needed the help of others and entrusted their plan to a few select convict friends who were also eager to escape. When a Dutch trading vessel arrived in Sydney, William became friends with the captain and had soon acquired a map, compass, a quadrant, two muskets and pork and rice which he secreted under the floorboards of his hut. Despite their best efforts to keep their escape a secret, their plan was discovered. David Collins, who was appointed the Judge-Advocate, wrote in his journal, *'overheard consulting in his hut after dark, with five other convicts, on the practicability of carrying off the boat in which he was employed. This circumstance being reported to the governor, it was determined that all his proceedings should be narrowly watched, and any scheme of that nature counteracted.'*

The very next day, whilst William was carrying out his duties of catching fish for the colony, the cutter was struck by a sudden squall. William and his crew had no choice but to abandon the boat and swim to shore. Collins then felt confident that any plans William might have had in escaping by boat was gone. His watch over him slackened. But Collins didn't bank on William and Mary's determination, and they continued collecting provisions for their escape. During this time, they accrued a fishing net, cooking utensils, hooks, nails, tents, flour, bedding, tools, fishing lines, rosin and a set of sails.

By now, William's sentence had expired, however, as the authorities had not been given any documentation of the expiry of the convicts' sentences there was no proof of this. Therefore, he continued to be treated as a convict serving his time. Private John Easty commented on this predicament *'they are the same as slaves all the time they are in this country although thare* [sic] *times for which they are sentenced are expired by law there is no difference between them and a convict that is jest cast for transportation.*' Mary must have felt a deep frustration when she saw her husband – a free man being treated as a slave - the look of hunger in the faces of her children and the deep lacerated scars across her husband's back. They must have felt that their situation would never change, and they would be worked to their death.

They bided their time until the perfect opportunity presented itself. The *Supply* was the only ship left in the colony after the *Sirius* had been wrecked at Norfolk Island in March 1790. A year later, the governor decided to send the *Supply* to Norfolk Island and a visiting Dutch vessel called the *Snow* had left the colony that morning. If they made their escape now and got a good head start, there wouldn't be a vessel big enough to catch up with them. The time to go was now.

They waited till nightfall to make their move. William and his crew were on fishing duty. There was no moon that night as one of the men slipped down to the government's cutter and untied it from the jetty. As quietly as they could, they hastily grabbed the provisions they had collected and piled them onboard the cutter. Mary carried her sleepy baby and urged her daughter to quickly make her way through to the boat without making a sound. Her heart must have been pounding inside her chest, willing little Emanuel not to cry out. With everyone on board they pushed out and began sailing the cutter out of the harbour.

Besides Mary, William and their two children aged just one and three years old, were William Allen, James Cox and Nathanial Lilley, who all held life sentences. There was also Samuel Bird, William Morton, James Martin and John Butcher. Morton was a navigator and at least Allen and Cox had experience with boats.

At daybreak they were discovered missing. David Collins noted, *'They were traced from Bryant's hut to the Point, and in the path were found a hand-saw, a scale, and four or five pounds of rice, scattered about in different places, which, it was evident, they had dropped in their haste.'* On closer inspection of Mary and William's hut authorities discovered a hidey hole under the floorboards. They also uncovered a well-hidden letter from James Cox to his girlfriend Sarah Young which outlined that he was leaving all his belongings to her.

By now the escapees were well out of the harbour and in open waters. They had secured the head start that they so desperately needed to make their escape. Their plan was to make their way to Timor, create new identities and get the next passing ship back to England as free people. Although the idea of making it to Timor in a cutter seemed impossible, similar feats had been accomplished. It was a huge risk but one they felt worthy of taking, and so began the mammoth task of inching their way up the east coast of Australia.

Along the way they needed to regularly pull into beaches to collect fresh water and patch up the boat. These early stops were such moments of joy as they felt truly free for the first time in their lives. They would bask in the sun during the day, catch fish and cure them. At night they would light a fire and sit around it, cooking their supper and imagining what their new lives would entail. They would entertain each other by inventing their new names and characters with interesting backstories. As wonderful as it was to dream, there must have been a niggling fear that Charlotte would give them away by mistake. She was only a toddler after all and could easily slip up. This would have added to Mary's worries and placed a lot more pressure on her as it would have been her role to keep her daughter close and prevent her from giving their real identities away.

Occasionally they would run into danger with the natives, but also had very positive encounters with them. On one occasion after spending two or three days in the little boat during a heavy storm they made it to shore and chanced upon two Aboriginal women with two children. As they approached them the women and children ran off terrified. The escapees motioned that they needed a light for a fire and the two women obliged. However, the following morning at about 11 o'clock a large group of Indigenous Australians approached them. The escapees were alarmed so they fired their musket above their heads and the group ran off. These encounters taught them to always be on guard and ready to launch the boat back out to sea.

They also faced dreadful storms that would leave them soaked to the bone. Because of the rain they couldn't even light a fire to warm their weary bodies and were forced to eat raw rice. Beaching and launching the boat wasn't an easy feat either. One time they were driven out to sea without being able to catch a glimpse of land for three weeks. But through all these difficulties they did have some extraordinary moments of wonder such as watching turtles coming to the shore to lay their eggs.

Although it is not known with any certainty which particular beaches they stopped at, it is thought that maybe Newcastle, Port Stephens and Moreton Bay were among them. It is also thought that they may have stopped at Lady

Elliot Island, on the southern tip of the Great Barrier Reef, as they were reported to have feasted on turtle and a fruit growing on the island. They stayed there for six days and one night, during which there was such a huge downpour they managed to collect two kegs of rainwater by using their sail. From there they island hopped hoping to find more turtles, but none were to be found.

As they rounded Cape York, they began the most perilous leg of their journey. As soon as they were in the Gulf of Carpentaria, they encountered a group of natives that are believed to have been Torres Strait Islanders. Mary and her crew became alarmed when they canoed towards them with what looked to be aggressive body language. They fired their musket once in response to scare them off, but this only aggravated the situation as the natives retaliated by firing arrows at them. Fortunately, none of the arrows reached their boat.

They continued to sail along. They were now desperate for water so had no choice but to come ashore again. They managed to find a deserted spot and filled up, but didn't want to risk spending the night there so returned to the safety of their boat. In the morning they started to return to land again to get more water, but this time they were spotted. James Martin described the scene, '*we saw two very large Canoes coming towards us we did not know what to do for we were Afraid to meet them there seemed to us to be 30 or 40 Men in each Canoe, they had Sails in their Canoes seemed to made of Matting one of their Canoes was a Head of the others a little Way Stopt untill the other Came up & then she Hoisted her Sails & made after us as soon as we saw that we Tack'd about with what Water we had - Determined to cross the gulf which was about five Hundred Miles Across which as God wou'd have it we out run them they followed us untill we lost sight of them.'*

They risked one more stop to stock up before embarking on the 500 mile treacherous journey to Timor. On 5 June they finally spotted land and pulled into a Dutch settlement in Koepang. Their epic journey had taken 69 days and they had travelled roughly 3,254 miles! They staggered into the small settlement, thoroughly exhausted and half starved. William wrote that Mary and the children had borne *'their suffering with more fortitude than any among them.'* Despite their weariness and fatigue, they all had to be alert as the Dutch authorities began questioning them. It was crucial that they remembered their stories.

They told the authorities that William Bryant was friends of a whale fisher, the ship had gone down and they were the only survivors. The governor believed their story and fed and clothed them. This was not the first time a boatload of English people had arrived on their shores. The first had been Bligh who had been cast adrift by bounty mutineers and travelled the same distance in an open boat. This incredible journey may well have inspired Mary and her group.

They quickly slotted into life in the settlement, even getting jobs, and lived quite happily. But as Watkin Tench described it *'their behaviour giving rise to suspicion, they were watched; and one of them at last, in a moment of intoxication, betrayed the secret.'* That person was William Bryant. Martin recorded, *'we remained very happy for two Months till Wm Bryant had words with his Wife who went and informed against himself, wife, Children and all of us; we were immediately taken prisoners and was put in the Castle.'* Despite repeatedly denying Bryant's drunken slip they were put into confinement. However, they were still given some freedoms. Martin claimed that they were *'allowed to go out of the Castle 2 at a time for one Day and the Next Day 2 more and so we Continued'*. That was until Captain Edwards arrived in the settlement.

Captain Edwards was a British naval officer who arrived in the settlement with a band of mutineers he was delivering back to England. Once he had secured the mutineers safely in the castle, he began his interrogation of Mary and her party. According to a man named Basil Thomson, Edwards *'was a cold, hard man devoid of sympathy and imagination'*. Eventually, one of them broke and confessed that they were convicts and divulged where they had come from. On 5 October, 1791, they boarded the *Rembang*. Martin claimed that Edwards *'put both our legs in irons called the Bilboes.'* A bilboe was a long iron bar with sliding shackles attached to it which was fastened to the floor. For the first time in years the convicts were shackled around the ankles.

They sailed to Batavia arriving on 7 November having survived a dreadful storm. They arrived in a weary, bedraggled state. Batavia was nothing like the island paradise they had just left. Batavia was renowned as a disease infested settlement. The death toll was extremely high for many visiting ships and those people that were lucky enough to escape with their lives left incredibly ill. Captain Cook described it in December 1770, *'Batavia is certainly a place that Europeans need not covet to go to, but, if necessity obliges them, they will do well to make their stay as short as possible, otherwise they will soon feel the effects of the unwholesome air of Batavia which, I firmly believe, is the death of more Europeans than any other place'*. Sadly, their visit was no different and on 1 December Mary's little baby boy Emanuel died, followed by her husband 21 days later.

The loss of her beloved husband and 20-month-old baby boy hit her incredibly hard, and she slipped into a depressed state. The fire inside her that had helped get them from Sydney to Timor had left her. To make matters worse, she, along with her daughter Charlotte and William Allen, were separated from the other men that had become like family to her. They were put on a ship called the *Horssen* and the other men were taken to the *Hoornwey*.

They set sail again with many still suffering from the unhealthy conditions at Batavia. As they were sailing through Sunda Strait, James Cox, one of her husband's closest friends, either fell overboard or decided to jump and was never seen again. William Morton also succumbed to the *'unwholesome air'* of Batavia. It was another huge blow to Mary.

On 18 March 1792 they arrived at Table Bay and five days later Mary, Charlotte and William Allen were transferred to another ship, the *Gorgon*. Days later they were happily reunited with the other escapees. It must have felt strange being on the *Gorgon,* as the ship had come from Australia and was crowded with reminders of their past – kangaroos, Australian animal skins, plants and shrubs. Plus, there were so many familiar faces as many marines that served in the colony were on the ship. Martin remarked, '*we was known well by all the marine officers which was all Glad that we had not perished at sea*'. Watkin Tench wrote, '*I confess that I never looked at these people without pity and astonishment. They had miscarried in a heroic struggle for liberty after having combated every hardship and conquered every difficulty ... I could not but reflect with admiration at the strange combination of circumstances which had again brought us together, to baffle human foresight and confound human speculation.*'

They sailed for Portsmouth on 5 or 6 of April. Two weeks into their journey the weather became scorching, and the intense heat brought about the death of many of the children of the marines. A total of seven children died. Then on the afternoon of 6 May Charlotte lost her life. A distraught Mary committed her little lifeless body to the deep dark sea. Mary now had nothing to live for. She had lost everything.

When they arrived in Portsmouth on 18 June, Mary was deep in her grief. She was returning to the shores of England after five years with nothing and still a prisoner. Her and her travel companions were thrown into Newgate prison to await their fate. Newgate was an unimaginably putrid prison. Gaol fever was rife in the overcrowded, confined spaces. A newspaper reported that the magistrate who committed them to Newgate had said, *'he never experienced so disagreeable a task as being obliged to commit them to prison, and assured them that, as far as lay in his power, he would assist them'*. However, despite the clemency of the crown the court was quite severe and sentenced them *'to remain on their former sentences until they should be discharged by due course of law'*.

The newspapers couldn't get enough of Mary's story and her plight and frequently wrote about her, drumming up huge sympathy from their readers. The *Dublin Chronicle* wrote on 21 July 1792, *'This escape was perhaps, the most hazardous and wonderful effort ever made by nine persons (for two were infants) to regain their liberty'*. One such reader, James Boswell, a lawyer who was known for successfully fighting for seemingly lost causes, decided to fight on Mary's behalf. He appealed to the Home Office for clemency and, using his connections, eventually secured a pardon for Mary. It was granted on 2 May 1793 – six weeks after her original sentence had expired.

Mary was now a free woman. She could scarcely believe it. But surprisingly she did not rush back to Cornwall to be with her family. Despite her release she was severely depressed. Her freedom must have felt bittersweet with no William, Charlotte or Emanuel to enjoy it with. She ended up staying in London until October when James finally convinced her to return home. He had written to her sisters who had assured him that Mary would be welcomed back with open arms. He not only paid for her passage home but promised her he would send her a monthly allowance *'as long as she behaved well'*. He also wanted to hear how she was doing. As she could not write, they agreed that she would get others to write on her behalf and she would sign it with her initials. This agreement was honoured.

James continued to fight for the freedom of Mary's companions; now only four of them remained. He couldn't have been more dedicated. One night when he was returning home he was accosted, robbed, and left unconscious. The violent assault left him bedridden, but even from his bed, and only nine days after the attack, he wrote again on their behalf and managed to secure their freedom. In November that year they too were released.

Mary and her friends had no way of ever repaying James for all that he had done for them. All they had between them were a few wild sarsaparilla tea leaves they had picked in the colony and brought with them on their extraordinary journey. James accepted the heartfelt gift and treasured it. He never used them, but kept them as a memento, and two of those precious leaves are now sitting in the Mitchell Library, Sydney having made their way back to their homeland.

All the escapees went on to lead very quiet lives. John Butcher, returned to New South Wales by enlisting in the New South Wales Corps. As a private he was granted land on 5 September 1795. As for Mary, she disappears into obscurity. It is thought that she eventually remarried.

The Cooking Pot Riot

What to do with reoffending convicts had always been a topic of hot debate. Punish them with physical pain such as flogging and irons, deprive them of everything in a solitary confinement cell or perhaps banish them from society again? In the early 1800s the government was so exasperated with the burden of convicts they were open to hearing any suggestions on the subject. In fact, Captain Maconochie was commissioned by the Prison Disciplinary Society to give his thoughts on reoffending convicts. Maconochie was the Lieutenant Governor of Van Diemen's Land. He had long given the subject thought and eagerly wrote his report, which was sent to the Colonial Office in October 1837. His ideas were to become known as the 'Mark System'.

The Mark System was a currency in which the criminal repaid his debt in marks and the size of the debt was dependent on the severity of the crime. The criminal could earn marks with good behaviour and task work. Maconochie wanted fixed term sentences abolished in replacement of this system. A criminal according to Maconochie was a *'debtor required to be imprisoned, or otherwise detained, till his debt is paid'*. He believed this gave the convict a purpose in life that would continue after the debt was repaid. Instead of physical punishments such as flogging and irons the convict would lose marks. Convicts were incentivised to earn marks and could use them to obtain better food and luxuries, though this wouldn't help them save enough marks to achieve their freedom. Maconochie believed this system would teach them the economics of looking after themselves in the real world.

There were many stages to the Mark System. The first, was a short stage of hard labour with moral, religious, and practical guidance. The next was working in small teams where everyone had their marks put into a collective pot. If one person lost marks for bad behaviour the whole team lost marks. '[G]*ood conduct popular, and misconduct unpopular, in the community, each affecting others as well as the individual actor*'. He believed this created a sense of social consciousness and community. Officials were so intrigued by his report he was given the go ahead to introduce it to Norfolk Island between 1840 – 1844.

From 1825 Norfolk Island had been a dumping ground for convicts who were considered the hardest reoffending criminals in the colony. Before Maconochie arrived, the convicts had been treated with such brutality it was almost considered inhumane even by the day's standards. From 1840, with the end of transportation to New South Wales, Norfolk Island's hotbed of notorious criminals had been diluted with fresh first-time offenders that were sent straight to the island from England. Maconochie was given instruction to keep these newcomers away from the old hands for fear of them being corrupted. But within a week he realised that given the small size of the island this would be impossible and abandoned the request.

Some of the luxuries that Maconochie introduced were a library and musical instruments. Maconochie also gave deserving convicts cooking pots and utensils to cook their own food. He allocated them small plots of land in which to cultivate their own vegetables to supplement their limited and dull rations. They were encouraged to rear livestock and grow tobacco and could trade these items. He shortened their workday and gave holidays for good behaviour. On Queen Victoria's birthday the convicts were treated to a day off and enjoyed the festivities such as team games and watched a theatre production put on by a group of convicts. They enjoyed fresh meat and drank rum. Unfortunately, Maconochie's festivities were mocked by the colonial press, who seemed to have it in for him, and the powers that be considered the Mark System to be a failure. He was replaced by Major Childs in February 1844.

Major Childs was a military man who had the reputation of being a strict disciplinarian. Once Major Childs was installed at Norfolk Island, he began stripping the convicts of the luxuries they had worked earnestly for. Over the next two years work hours were lengthened, rations were reduced and brutal punishments such as flogging were regularly handed down. They also lost their garden plots that they had worked so hard to cultivate. With each privilege that was ripped away from them the convicts grew more and more resentful and bitter. Most of the convicts already despised authority but this just escalated their hatred. Their anger began brewing and fermenting like a pustulous boil waiting to erupt.

When the convicts awoke on the morning of 1 July 1846, they discovered that their cooking utensils had been confiscated during the night and when they demanded to know where they were, they were informed that they wouldn't be needing them any longer as they were no longer free to cook for themselves. This was the final straw.

It was a convict by the name of William Westwood that took the lead. Westwood was better known as 'Jackey Jackey the gentleman bushranger' a notorious reoffender. He had originally been sentenced to 14 years transportation for stealing a coat. Once he was in the colony, he was assigned to an overseer in Bungendore that treated him badly by not giving him enough food to eat and not supplying him with clothing. This led Westwood to steal wheat, he was caught, imprisoned, and returned to the overseer. Westwood escaped and roamed the southern district, stealing all that he needed to survive in the bush – horses, clothes, food, arms, and money. He was known as the gentleman bushranger as he never harmed his victims, and he was courteous with women.

After years of brutal treatment and this last semblance of human decency being denied them, something snapped inside Westwood. He turned to his fellow prisoner, Lawrence Kavanagh, another renowned bushranger, and together they led a group of angry men to rush the stores and reclaim their cooking utensils. With anger still coursing through their bodies, they charged towards the constables' barracks. They broke into the barracks, smashing windows and severely beating any officers they came across. They seized the officers' cooking pots and pans, bashing them around until they were destroyed. The riot was now in full swing and growing in numbers and strength.

The prisoners returned to the mess room and killed a gatekeeper named John Morris before storming the cook house and brutally slaughtering an officer named Stephen Smith. The group was out of control, and they intended to kill every free person on the island. They continued their murderous rampage, heading to the lime kiln hut where three constables lay sleeping in their beds after working on night duty. Two of the constables received fatal blows to the head with an axe but the third, Michael Ryan, awoke to the noise and managed to escape outside, where he was met by Westwood who nearly bludgeoned him to death. Another prisoner managed to talk Westwood down and saved Ryan from a terrible death. Ryan was left critically injured.

By this time the military had been notified of the riot and were hot on their heels. To the relief of the free settlers the military were quickly able to surround the prisoners. Around 1,100 prisoners were secured in the yard. Each prisoner was inspected and any showing splatters of blood on them were placed to one side and secured in irons, then locked in various government buildings around the island. Westwood walked up to the Major, his face, hands and shirt covered in blood, and said, '*I suppose it's me you want.*' He and Kavanagh were taken to the boathouse where they were shackled to a cable.

Knowing that they would all be hanged for their actions numerous escapes were attempted, with six men nearly succeeding. They had somehow obtained a chisel, a notched knife and a file and set to work trying to free themselves from their handcuffs. To cover the sound, they sang a favourite song that went:

'*Merry row, merry row,*
My bonnie, bonnie bark,
Bring back my love to calm my woe,
Before the night grows dark.'

The prisoners did manage to free themselves of their handcuffs, however, were caught when a fellow prisoner betrayed them. This led to the guard being doubled. Another group of prisoners continued their assault by tossing stones at the guards, which led to the guards firing at them with two being seriously wounded.

The gruesome, bloody attack shook every free settler on the island, particularly the women, and it wasn't long before many of them had packed up all their belongings and were boarding the next ship off the island. Several government men also resigned their positions and left the island, feeling that they were doomed if they stayed, so great was the hatred felt by the prisoners.

On 13 October 12 men were brought up to the scaffold. They had been sentenced to death for their murderous rampage. Two other men had been lucky enough to be acquitted. Westwood, Henry Whiting, and William Pickthorne received counsel by the Reverend Mr Rogers. The other nine men, who were of the Roman Catholic faith, were attended by Reverends Murray & Bond. In his last moments Westwood made a desperate plea to Reverend Rogers saying, *'I wish to say, as a dying man, that I believe four men now going to suffer, are innocent of the crime now laid to their charge, viz.—Lawrence Kavenagh, Henry Whiting, William Pickthorne, and William Scrimshaw, and declare that I never spoke to Kavenagh on the morning of the riots; and these other three men had no part in the killing of John Morris, as far as I know of.'* Two of the three men swore they were innocent, but it fell on deaf ears.

Westwood didn't deny his involvement in the crimes. As his last act, before the noose was tightened around his neck, Westwood placed a written history of his life into the hands of Reverend Rogers. Westwood was only 26 years old at the time of his execution.

Neva – One of the Worst Shipwrecks in Australian History

They were 125 days into the voyage. They left Cork in Ireland on 8 January 1835 and so far it had been a fairly uneventful trip. Bound for Sydney under the command of Captain Benjamin Peck were 150 female convicts along with 33 of their children, nine free women with their 22 children and a crew of 26. The prisoners were kept away from the free women as much as possible. The Superintendent Surgeon John Stephenson, who was in charge of the convicts, had settled the convict women into a routine. The weather had been fair, so the women had spent a lot of their time on the upper deck. When they weren't engaged in the tasks of scrubbing the decks, washing the clothes, and cleaning the prison below, there was sewing and needlework to pass the time.

The women had been divided into messes of eight with one of the group made head mess or matron. These women were hand-picked by the surgeon and were usually chosen for their good behaviour noted in the reports from the Governor of Cork. Each mess was assigned to one berth and shared drinking vessels and wooden platters which were marked with the number of their mess. Two or three convicts were chosen to be the cooks for all the convict women. They probably worked under the supervision of a head cook. The days came and went in relative calm, but lately there was a sense that the journey was coming to an end.

The crew had been split into two groups called watches,

rotating their deck duties to keep the ship sailing. Each shift was between two and four hours long. The crew had to keep the ship operating at maximum efficiency and they were always busy adjusting the sails to take advantage of the direction of the wind. Ideally the ship would be downwind, with the wind coming from behind, propelling them forward. But if they needed to head straight into the wind the crew would lead the ship into the wind at angles, this was known as 'tacking into the wind'. The captain kept the crew very busy for two reasons – firstly, there was always so much to do and they needed to be hypervigilant to any changes of wind speed and direction and, secondly, because he feared that idle crew might lead to mutiny which had happened on other ships. When not adjusting the sails, the crew were checking that the hull and rigging were in good order, or they were scraping the rust off chain cables.

At midday on 12 May the three-masted barque was rounding the southern point of the Australian mainland and heading into the treacherous waters of Bass Strait. King Island was 90 miles to the west of them. Peck was an experienced master and had sailed the *Neva* to Port Jackson about two years prior. Having spent those four months sailing her from Plymouth he knew her every quirk. From the way she heaved under sail to the rolling waves, to the sound of the whistle in her ropes and the creaks made under his feet as he charged from one end of her to the other. Every ship had its own soul, and a deep connection was formed by her seamen.

At 2 a.m. the wind picked up and King Island was spotted. Peck felt confident in his calculations and by the light of the moon he steered the *Neva* port tack to keep clear of the Harbinger Reefs. They continued this way for the next three hours until the lookout cried out that there were breakers ahead. Peck instantly responded by ordering the helm hard a-starboard. But as the *Neva* turned, her keel struck a rock and came away. Peck navigated her back into the wind again but struck the reef on the port bow and swung broadside on. The crew did everything they could, but the ship began filling with water. The foremasts and top masts were cut away, but the posts holding up the prison walls collapsed in, causing the prisoners to scramble up to the top deck.

The crew now began to launch the lifeboats, however, when they were preparing the gig, in their haste, the iron davit broke and the gig fell into pieces. They swiftly began untying the next boat and lowering it down into the sea. On board this pinnace was Captain Peck, a very ill Stephenson, who had been suffering from scorbutic dysentery, and a handful of crew and prisoners. But the women left behind, in their growing panic rushed the small boat and it sank. Unfortunately, everyone in the little boat drowned apart from the captain and two of the seamen. The longboat and the cutter were the next boats to be launched but they were both capsized by the crashing waves.

Four hours had now passed since the *Neva* had crashed into the rock. Some of the women had helped themselves to the liquor in the cuddy and were hopelessly drunk when the ship began to break into pieces from the pounding waves. The poop deck caved in on top of the women, killing most inside the cuddy. Many of those who weren't killed were too drunk to save themselves and perished. As the ship broke apart the people left on board fell straight into the cold water and struggled to stay afloat. Sadly, most people couldn't swim and were swept away and drowned. Others scrambled to grab hold of debris that had floated to the surface. Captain Peck and around 20 other people held onto one piece of the ship, but with each wave crashing down upon them, after eight hours of drifting, only Peck and two others remained.

Over the next eight long hours 22 men and women survivors drifted to shore still clinging to pieces of the wreckage. They stumbled out of the water utterly depleted and collapsed in a heap. Amongst them were Captain Peck, chief mate Joseph Bennett, 12 female prisoners and eight of the crew. They looked around and discovered a barrel of rum had washed to shore. Peck served each survivor a dram of the rum to warm and comfort themselves a little. They soon fell into an exhausted sleep in the nearby bush. When Peck awoke, he was dismayed to find many of them had died during the night and strangely some of them were found face down in the sand in different locations. He concluded that they must have died of cold and fatigue. There were now only 15 survivors.

In the coming days various bits and pieces from the ship drifted to shore. The survivors collected whatever was useful for them and were overjoyed when barrels of flour and pork washed ashore. But debris and supplies weren't the only thing that reached them. Up and down the beach they were confronted by the horrifying sight of the dead bodies of the people with whom they had spent the last few months. Over the course of two days Peck and his crew buried 95 bodies. Dejected and weak they waited out their time, rationing their supplies and praying that a passing ship would rescue them. They had no way of letting anyone know what had happened to them and where they were. They were banking on a miracle.

Two weeks had passed, and they were surely feeling hopeless. They were faced with the very real possibility that might slowly die on this deserted beach on the other side of the world from their loved ones. That was until they saw two men walking towards them! They could scarcely believe what they were seeing. The group met the men with jubilation, thinking that they had been saved, but to their bitter disappointment the men had been marooned also. They soon learned that the ship these men had been travelling on called the *Tartar* had been wrecked at about the same time as the *Neva*. The men told them of a man named Scott who worked as a sealer and lived on the island. Together they went to Scott's hut. Scott owned several dogs and used them to capture wallabies to feed all the survivors.

Not long after meeting Scott, Charles Friend, the owner of the *Tartar,* arrived on the island looking for his ship. Upon hearing of the loss of his ship and the loss of the *Neva* he trekked to Peck's camp. After rounding up the survivors and putting them on his small vessel, he set sail. Unfortunately, three survivors were on another part of the island and had to be left behind. He promised that he would send another boat out for them later. Friend and his boatload of survivors arrived in George Town, on the Tamar River near Launceston on 26 June. It had been more than six weeks since the *Neva* had been wrecked and, true to his word, a government vessel was sent back to King Island to rescue the two women and the man that was left behind.

An enquiry was held later over the loss of the ship and so many lives. In his evidence, Peck put the accident down to the strong current pulling the ship southward and the incorrect positioning of the Harbinger Reef on his map. The court exonerated Peck, Surgeon Stephenson, the officers and all the crew of all responsibility for the loss. The court decided that the loss came down to *'the reef being improperly laid down or an erroneous opinion formed by the master and crew of their distance from the land when the ship hauled to the wind, or more probably the concurrent influence of several minute errors'.*

There has been some confusion over the exact number of lives lost. According to Captain Peck 218 people drowned that day. 138 were convicts. There were also another seven people who died after reaching King Island. Six of the seven were convicts, bringing the total loss of life to 225 people, 144 of those were convicts, 55 of them were children – making it one of the worst shipwrecks in Australian history.

Australia's First Bank Robbery

It was a crisp Monday morning in Spring 1828 when the bank teller descended the stairs into the basement room of the Bank of Australia. The doors of the bank, located in George Street Sydney, had not yet opened for business. As he made his way downstairs, he could hear the other bank tellers busily preparing for business above him. He didn't bother with a light as he had left the float in a spot before he clocked off late Saturday night. A spot that was easily reached in the dark. He knew the building well by now and had made this same movement countless times. It was his daily routine. He reached out and placed his hand on the spot where he had left the money, and his heart skipped a beat as his hand failed to locate the bag. In a panic he groped around and felt the blood drain from his body. Adrenaline kicked in and he scurried to light the room. When the room came into view, he hurriedly looked about hoping that the money had fallen to the ground, but to his horror he discovered that the room was in disarray and there was a hole in the foundation wall. The bank had been robbed!

In no time at all the directors and police had been notified and news of the robbery began sweeping through the town of Sydney. A thorough search of the strong room was conducted and revealed that around £14,000 had been stolen in bank notes, British silver coins and Spanish dollars. That's about 20 million dollars by today's standards. The robbers had left behind large quantities of gold and the bulk of the silver coins, and it was assumed that they were too heavy for the thieves to carry away.

Upon investigation of the hole that had been chiselled through the nine feet thick foundation wall, police discovered that it led to a drain that ran from Essex Street, under George Street, under Redman's Pub to Sydney Cove. In it was a trail of things that the robbers had left behind. This included a crowbar, a sword saw, a sounder, a tinder box and steel, a broken lantern, a lamp and a bottle of oil, some empty bottles of rum and a gill measure. There was also a trail of coins.

The town was abuzz with excitement about the discovery. Sydneysiders were astonished that thieves could have pulled off such a huge heist. It was all anyone was talking about. If you had somehow not heard about it through the grapevine, then you read about it on the front page in the newspaper. What had everyone talking was the reward of £100 offered by the directors of the bank. People began questioning if they had seen something and rumours were rife.

Naturally, the authorities were quick to suspect a convict was guilty of the crime. Just two days after the discovery of the missing fortune the *Sydney Gazette* published a proclamation from the Governor, Ralph Darling, on the front page promising an Absolute Pardon to any prisoner of the Crown who came forward with information that would lead to the discovery and conviction of the robbers. They surmised that it had to be a group of thieves and owing to the tools that were needed to carry out such a job they brought in a number of stonemasons for questioning.

The directors of the bank were so desperate for the money to be returned they took further measures to try and catch the thieves. A few days after the robbery they released new notes and gave the public a window of opportunity to bring in their old notes in exchange for the new ones. The public was warned not to accept payment with old notes. On top of the £100 reward for any information resulting in the apprehension and conviction of the robbers, the directors also offered free passage to England for the informant.

As enticing as these rewards were, police were still no closer to capturing the offenders. On 24 September, the Board of Directors published in the *Sydney Gazette* the list of numbers of the £50 notes that were stolen, cautioning the public not to accept these notes for payment. They also increased the reward again. Along with an Absolute Pardon, £100 reward and a free passage to England they offered the informant five percent of the total amount recovered in stolen money.

Two days later, £150 of the stolen money was found concealed in an outhouse in a yard in Cumberland Street. *The Australian* newspaper reported that police were questioning 10 individuals about it. But after extensive questioning no charges were laid. There simply was not enough evidence to make an arrest.

More than two years passed without police being any closer to solving the mystery. Until finally one of the thieves came forward and confessed. His name was William Blackstone. He had been transported to Australia with a sentence of 14 years and arrived on board the *Mariner*. Blackstone had been in and out of trouble since his arrival and had several stints in the penal settlement in Newcastle and felt the lash across his back. He was considered to be a 'bad character' by authorities. After robbing the bank, he had found himself in trouble again and was sent to the notorious Norfolk Island. He was so desperate to get away that he was glad to be chosen as a witness in the Adam Oliver murder trial and sent to Sydney. But faced with returning to Norfolk Island and the anger he felt at his accomplices for not giving him his cut of the loot, when pressed, he confessed his part in the bank robbery and gave up everyone who was involved. To turn snitch made you the lowest of the low amongst convicts but he wanted revenge for their betrayal.

Blackstone stood before Mr Justice Dowling and the jury on Friday, 10 June 1831. As Blackstone began to answer questions the jury took in his brown hair and hazel eyes, his heavily tattooed arms, and his rather generously proportioned nose. He was a man that you didn't forget in a hurry. Blackstone's story began in mid-August when two fellow convicts named Dingle and Farrell came to his house one night and shared with him their plan to rob the Bank of Australia. At that time, Blackstone had only been in Sydney for six months and claimed not to have even known where the bank was.

James Dingle was a shoemaker from Dublin who had been transported in 1815 on the *Dorothy* with a sentence of seven years for stealing. Nearly two years prior to the robbery Dingle had earned himself a Certificate of Freedom. He had been in his late twenties when he arrived at Blackstone's house that fateful night. With his young friend George Farrell in tow, he tossed a small stone onto the roof of the house to attract Blackstone's attention. Farrell was also from Dublin and had been sentenced to seven years for theft. Farrell had been in and out of trouble since his arrival in 1822. He'd experienced many of the punishments that the courts had to offer. He'd done time on the treadmill, been worked in leg irons for three months and after being discovered drunk and disorderly, had lost his privilege of being able to sleep outside of the Barracks.

Blackstone listened as Dingle described his plan for breaking into the bank. Dingle had assured him it could be done, as he had it on good authority from his mate Thomas Turner – a convict who had been employed to build the strong room of the bank - that it could be breached by tunnelling through a drain. He admitted that he was sceptical at first but later agreed after Dingle's persuasive arguments. Dingle then gave him a list of tools that he needed Blackstone to make in order to drill into the wall of the bank.

According to Blackstone it took roughly a week to come up with the tools and then the three men agreed to meet at 4 a.m. one morning to measure out the drain and where they would need to start tunnelling. The wall was about nine feet thick, so they wanted to get it right. They crept silently passed Mr Redman's house, careful not to wake anyone up, and dashed stealthily across his backyard to the drain. After lowering themselves inside they lit their lantern and quietly slid their feet through the mud. Locating the spot where they were to start tunnelling, Blackstone placed some bricks in the mud so they could stand on them whilst working. They chipped away at the drain all day and made their exit once it was growing dark. They slipped out of the drain at another exit in Mr Thornton's paddock which lay opposite the bank.

The following week they met again but this time Blackstone was alarmed to see that Dingle and Farrell had not come alone. They had brought their friend John Creighton with them. Dingle reassured Blackstone that Creighton would be an asset as he was the one who had laid the floor of the strong room. Reluctantly, Blackstone proceeded with

Creighton into the drain and began work as the other two stayed outside and kept watch. They worked steadily throughout that Saturday and trudged out into the daylight that afternoon, where they informed Dingle and Farrell that they were only one day away from breaking into the bank, but would have to wait until next Saturday to break through. Dingle wouldn't hear of it. He wanted them to meet the following day, but Blackstone pointed out that he and Farrell had to be at church muster.

Dingle took a deep breath and thought about it for a moment. He was desperate to crack through that wall. They were so close he could almost feel the money in his hands. But what to do about the muster? If Blackstone and Farrell weren't there for the count, they would be punished, which could mean waiting even longer. Suddenly an idea popped into his mind! Dingle was mates with the clerk and could ask him if he could excuse Blackstone and Farrell from church muster. He relayed his idea to the others and told them to start work tomorrow morning. If Dingle could arrange to get them exempted *'he would throw a handful of coppers down the grating as a signal'*. The men agreed to meet the next morning.

Before daybreak the next day the men crept silently through the streets of Sydney, meeting at the entrance to the drain. There Blackstone, Farrell and Creighton slipped into the drain leaving Dingle outside. Dingle had his own tasks to complete before the men broke the wall of the bank. Not only did he have to get Blackstone and Farrell the pass to miss church muster, but he also had to find a way of getting the people he lived with out of the house that night as the men had agreed that the safest place to take their booty was to Dingle's place.

Only 20 minutes after the men started into the drain,

they heard the sound of someone approaching them. They immediately stopped what they were doing, hoping that it was Dingle, and called out *'who's there?'*. *'Val Rourke'* came the answer. *'Who sent you'* they cried. Rourke approached the men and told them he had been sent by Dingle. Blackstone was outraged! He could not believe Dingle had told yet another person, and fearing that he would get caught he said he would have nothing more to do with it and turned to leave. Rourke assured him that he could keep his mouth shut. Creighton and Farrell pleaded with Blackstone not to leave and pointed out that he had done most of the hard work – if any of them deserved a cut of the riches, it was him. Reluctantly Blackstone agreed and they carried on.

The four men took turns chiselling away until finally they reached the last stone into the vault. At that moment they heard the drums beat signalling it was time for church. Within moments Dingle threw the coppers into the drain. Excitedly, they took out the corner stone. They had made it through. They shone the light through the hole in the wall and quickly debated whether they should enter the bank now or at nightfall. They decided that the time was now.

Farrell was tasked with going through the hole in the wall. He was the youngest of the group, aged around 24, and was a much smaller build than the others, so it would be easier for him to climb through. Once inside he grabbed two ornate japanned tins and some small yellow canvas bags and came back through the hole to show the others what he had found. The japanned tins had locks, so the men broke them open. Inside were notes of various denominations. More money than they had ever seen. Inside the yellow bags were coins – half crowns and shillings. Farrell crawled through into the bank to retrieve more. This time he returned with a brown japanned tin and a small white tin, containing books without covers. When Creighton inspected the books, he found that they listed the numbers of the notes. They had to be destroyed, so the men took the papers and rubbed them into the muddy water sitting stagnate in the drain.

Again, Farrell went into the drain, passing through bags of coins and notes to Blackstone, who passed them to Rourke and Creighton so they could sort the money. They divided the notes into five parcels that were to be put into the hat of each man. This was to keep them off the wet floor of the drain and later so they could walk through town without raising suspicion. By the time they left the drain it was evening. They had taken all that they could manage, leaving behind more notes, silver coins, the broken boxes and the tools lying on the floor of the drain. As they headed out, they met Dingle who had come with some bags to help carry their loot. He told the men to head to his house and let themselves in through the backdoor which he had left unlocked. He had successfully got everyone out of the house for the evening and assured them they would not be disturbed. As the men set off, Dingle went into the drain to collect what coins he could.

Despite having stolen more money than they would make in their entire lives some were eager to go back and get more. Blackstone, however, wanted to get home and wash. He didn't want the people he lived with to notice any break from his usual routine, so he made to go. Not long after he returned home Dingle appeared and convinced him to meet them again later that night. So, when the house was quiet Blackstone slipped out, careful not to wake anybody, and headed back to the drain. Quietly, the men retraced their steps along the drain and plundered more money from the bank. On their way back they each took turns to climb the wall over Mr Thornton's paddock. When it was Blackstone's turn, he heard a constable questioning Dingle down the lane. Blackstone slid down the wall and instead of heading to Dingle's place he turned and went in the direction of home. He stashed the box of money he had been carrying under his arm and hid it amongst some stones, then slipped into his home without waking a soul and tried to get some sleep.

The next morning when Blackstone woke up his mind instantly went to the sequence of events that had occurred the previous night. He was convinced that Dingle and the other men had been apprehended by the constable. Blackstone tried to act as if nothing was remiss and went to his forge to start his duties as a blacksmith. As he worked on creating a new tool, he was surprised when he looked up and found Dingle standing in front of him. When he asked Dingle what had happened Dingle told him the constable had questioned him but, as he was a free man, he let him go. The other men had hidden behind the church with the booty. Blackstone and Dingle made plans to meet at Dingle's house with the money Blackstone had secreted and they would split the proceeds between all the men.

Once the money had been divided, Blackstone took a cut of it to a man named Woodward who he'd known for some time. Woodward was a convict who was known to be shady. He sold spirits, without a licence, on the side and was always up for making a quick buck. When Blackstone told him he had an offer for him, Woodward led him into a private room. There, Blackstone carefully unwrapped his silk handkerchief and revealed a large wad of notes. The bank robbery was yet to be discovered so Woodward had no idea how Blackstone had got his hands on so much money. There was over £1000 in the handkerchief. Blackstone explained that they had been stolen from the Bank of Australia but assured him that their numbers had been destroyed. Woodward agreed to exchange the money off him for a profit. Blackstone happily agreed to his terms and headed to muster at the racecourse.

As he approached the racecourse, he saw Farrell talking to Thomas Turner outside St James Church on Macquarie Street. He continued on and after discovering there was to be no muster that day, he headed down Phillip Street and was soon joined by Farrell. Blackstone asked Farrell what he had been discussing with Turner and Farrell told him he had given him some of the stolen money to keep him quiet. They headed to the public house and shared a drink before parting ways.

Blackstone returned to Woodward several times to collect his money but was met with excuse after excuse. Blackstone also approached Dingle for the rest of his cut. Dingle told him that he had been robbed on Parramatta Road but would go up country and get some of the cash for him, however he never saw the money. On 14 September, 1829, Blackstone became a free man but in November was arrested for highway robbery and sentenced to death, which was later commuted to 14 years transportation to Norfolk Island.

And there Blackstone's story of the events ended, and he paused as everyone in the jury took in what he had just relayed. Other witnesses were called, and evidence given that supported certain aspects of his version of events. The trial went into the night, and it wasn't until 10 o'clock that evening that the Judge began summing up. At half past 12 the jury retired and returned shortly thereafter with a guilty verdict for Dingle, Farrell and Woodward.

For weeks the barristers argued that the principal

witness – William Blackstone – was a convict and therefore his evidence was tainted. Arguments and counter arguments were hurled back and forth with the three presiding judges sitting back and contemplating each point. Until finally on 23 July 1831, six weeks after their trial, the three men were brought to court for the fourth time. Woodward was sentenced to 14 years transportation to a penal settlement and much to everyone's surprise Dingle and Farrell were saved from the hangman's noose and were given life sentences on Norfolk Island.

For the next six weeks Blackstone, Dingle, Farrell, and Woodward were all kept on the *Phoenix* hulk waiting for the orders to be processed. Presumably they were kept far apart from each other. On 1 September 1831, Blackstone was taken to the Hyde Park Barracks and given his Absolute Pardon and at some point, the directors of the bank handed him his £100 and a passport for free passage back to England. He should have got on the next ship but instead he decided to stay, and it wasn't long before he had reoffended and was back before the courts and sent to Norfolk Island where his former accomplices – Dingle and Farrell were.

The clerk, James John Wood, who saved Blackstone and Farrell from church muster that day argued that he should get the rewards as he had testified against them all at court. He was able to prove that Dingle was associated with Farrell and Blackstone that day. The directors denied his claim but ended up giving him £25 as his evidence did play a vital role in the case. He also made his case to British authorities and in 1833 was awarded a Conditional Pardon and later in 1836 an Absolute Pardon.

John Creighton was never arrested for the robbery because he died in a boating accident off South Head in

1829. His wife Ann, who lost not only her husband that terrible day but also her father, married Dingle later that year. In 1833, Dingle made his escape from Norfolk Island by piratically seizing a boat and was never seen again – he was presumed drowned. Poor Ann was made a widow again. Farrell also made several attempts at escape but was never successful. He was in and out of trouble for the rest of his life.

Valentine Rourke, perhaps the smartest of the lot, left the colony and headed to England on board the *Midas* soon after the robbery. The authorities sent a letter to England for his apprehension, but he was never found. And as for Thomas Turner it could never be proved that he had anything to do with the robbery, however his petitions for a Ticket of Leave were repeatedly ignored.

The money, to this day, has not been recovered in full. A child playing near a well discovered £2,959 hidden under a stone and was rewarded with £148, a small stash of £140 was found in the rafters of a public toilet in The Rocks and a bundle of £50 notes was discovered under a rock near Liverpool Street. In 1893, a woman went to the authorities claiming that her husband had confessed on his death bed that the money was hidden near Mrs Macquarie's Chair in the Domain, so the Premier, Sir George Dibbs authorised an excavation of the area, but nothing was ever found. Another theory comes from a night fisherman who claims that he saw a mysterious rower slipping in and out of Little Sirius Cove and other nearby coves around the time of the robbery. Could there be boxes of the spoils buried near the water's edge around the small bays on Sydney's north shore?

Ten Convicts Seize the *Frederick*

~

It was the evening of 13 January 1834 when two convicts named Shires and Leslie burst into the ship's cabin and levelled their pistols at Captain Taw and Mr Hoy, the shipwright. Shires exclaimed, *'We've got the vessel now, and if you don't give yourself up, I will blow your brains out'*. A scuffle broke out which left the captain with a gaping wound to his head. *'We have got every body secured ... it is of no use you and Mr Hoy contending against us'*, one of the convicts called out from the hatchway above. The convicts assured the captain that if he and the shipwright gave themselves up, they would not be killed. They also warned them against doing anything to sabotage their getaway such as breaking quadrants, compasses or anything else they might need for their escape. Realising they were outnumbered; the captain and Mr Hoy reluctantly surrendered.

The 10 armed convicts had now secured the ship. The *Frederick* was a new brig that hadn't been completed. Work began on the *Frederick* in a penal settlement on Sarah Island in Macquarie Harbour, Tasmania. The settlement had all but been abandoned, with the majority of convicts and officers being sent to Port Arthur. Only a skeletal crew were left behind to finish the *Frederick* and when it was complete, they were to sail it to Port Arthur. Only 12 convicts were kept behind employed as shipwrights and were later to act as crew when the vessel was set to sail. A great deal of trust was placed in the convicts, which was surprising considering that Sarah Island was a secondary punishment site largely made up of convicts who had tried to escape in the past. At the height of its occupation, it had 386 prisoners – mostly men. It was an incredibly isolated outpost, surrounded by uncharted dense wilderness and a river that met the sea in a narrow, dangerous channel that had been nicknamed by convicts as 'Hell's Gates'. Sarah Island had a fierce reputation as the most brutal secondary punishment site, with many going mad or choosing death rather than serve out another day there.

The convicts rounded up all their victims and forced them into the jolly boat ordering them to row to Wellington Head, the southern point of Macquarie Harbour. Along with Captain Taw and Mr Hoy there were four soldiers, a free man named James Tait and two convicts Nicholls and Macfarlane who had refused to join in on the mutiny. As they pulled away from the ship, four of the rebel convicts boarded the whaleboat and followed closely behind them with their muskets at the ready. When their boat was almost at the shore the convicts ordered the men out of the jolly boat. Having secured the jolly boat to the whaleboat the convicts set off leaving the men stranded, promising to return in the morning with provisions.

The castaways spent a restless night huddled together in the scrub, worried how they would survive and hoping that the convicts would return. To their relief, just as the sun was beginning to rise, they spotted some of the convicts rowing out to them. When they reached the beach, the convicts handed some provisions and cooking utensils to the castaways before quickly heading back to the *Frederick*. Shortly after daybreak they watched as the convicts sailed the *Frederick* past Hell's Gates and clear out to sea. James Porter, one of the convicts on board recalled, '*I cannot express my feelings at that moment my heart expanded* (!) *within me and I believe I could not feel happier*'.

Weeks of planning had gone into capturing the *Frederick* and they had to wait for the right time to strike. Barker, a convict working as a gunsmith in the settlement, had been secretly making them arms and stashing them away. With the weapons ready, they waited until an opportunity presented itself. They took their chance when two of the four soldiers decided to go fishing away from the vessel and without the permission of the captain. The remaining two soldiers were on deck unarmed. They had taken the ship quickly using the element of surprise.

Only four out of the 10 convicts had experience sailing and they were working with a ship that wasn't entirely ready for an open sea voyage. In fact, the ship was designed to hug coastlines and certainly wasn't built to battle the heavy seas of the Southern and Pacific oceans. The *Frederick* required a big, experienced crew to man it's sails. It had more sails than most ships and most of the sails were very worn. The main top sail was meant for a much smaller ship, and they had no square mainsail. The only new sail on board was the foresail. The ship was, however, well provisioned with food and tools. On board were three or four casks of Irish beef, a goat and a kid, dozens of ducks and fowls, three pigs, two geese and bags of flour, and quantities of biscuits, sugar, tea and even some spirits. Not to mention a tomcat for good luck. They also had the advantage of a huge head start. Captain Taw and his party would not be able to reach a settlement and send word of the seizure of the *Frederick* for weeks. The *Frederick* was also a fast-sailing vessel so it was highly unlikely that anyone would be able to catch up with them.

It was assumed that the convicts would sail to New Zealand, but they had much grander plans than that. They were going to make the epic journey to Chile. It was apparently Barker who suggested Chile. Chile was somewhere the authorities wouldn't suspect and it had recently gained its independence from Spain. The convicts would also be following the prevailing winds, making it easier to get there. They could sail south avoiding one of the busiest shipping lanes. Plus, James Porter had a wife and child in Chile whom he hadn't seen in about 15 years.

They started heading south south-west but within an hour or two of leaving Hell's Gates one of the men noticed a small leak. This wasn't unusual for a brand new ship. The planking needed time to settle – something this ship never got the chance to do. They hastily found the two pumps on board and put them to work, only to discover that one of the pumps wasn't functioning. The pumps hadn't been tested before the vessel was launched. Pumping water was a strenuous job for two men and with only one working pump they would never get on top of the leaking. The best they could hope for was to keep it at bay until they reached Chile.

As they headed further south a ferocious wind picked up, gaining strength by the hour. The ship began to be tossed about and the less experienced convicts were hit by a sudden seasickness that saw them take to their bunks, violently ill. The ship rode up the top of the waves stretched out before them like a monstruous mountain range and then came crashing down into the trough. It was a testament to James Hoy's shipbuilding skills that the *Frederick* did not break into pieces. As the men lay sick in their beds, the four experienced convicts did everything they could to man the ship through the turbulent sea, but they were severely shorthanded. With no able bodies to pump the water out of the hold it had quickly risen to waist height.

Once the storm had passed, they assessed the leak and agreed to have two men on the pump 24 hours a day. Each man did a two-hour shift. The sailors pushed the ship to breaking point, feeling an overwhelming sense of urgency to get to Chile, but also a sense of fear that they were somehow being closely followed. Though this was highly unlikely given the huge head start they had. They didn't have enough crew to work all the sails, so they downsized them making them easier to manage. Over the coming days the convicts fell into a routine, each with their own jobs, some performing them in between bouts of seasickness.

On 25 February, they finally spotted land. Though not all on board believed it was land. Barker thought it was a bank of cloud. However, as they drew nearer their hopes were realised. They had made the epic journey of more than 6,000 nautical miles to the coast of South America in about six weeks with just a handful of experienced men. Most voyages had at least seven times that many crew. What they had achieved was truly remarkable. The men were exhausted but euphoric.

The *Frederick* was now just limping along, gaining water at a fast pace. Its timbers groaned as it cut through the water. She had served them well but wouldn't make it for the last leg of the journey. Porter described her in his memoir, '*proud we were of it*'. The convicts began preparing to take the longboat. There was much work to be done to it. It needed to be rigged with a sail and refitted to allow room for all 10 of them. They transferred what food they had left into the longboat along with all the arms and ammunition. They weren't going to land just anywhere in Chile. They wanted to come ashore at the Port of Valdivia. By the time the 10 men and their cat boarded the longboat the water had reached the bulkhead and was rising fast. They were all sad to see her go. They had left all the hatches open so she would not break apart but gracefully subside into the depths of the ocean.

Crammed into the longboat they made their way closer to the land. The sea was angry, sending huge waves down upon them, drenching them and everything in the boat. They spent a very cold, wet, uncomfortable night and by morning they were freezing. They made a direct beeline for land, but it took them a while to find the right little cove that would provide shelter for their boat. It wasn't until late afternoon that they disembarked. It had been about six weeks since they had last felt solid ground underneath their feet. They stumbled out of the sea and onto dry sand and then explored the surrounding forest, trying to regain their land legs. They were disappointed not to find any signs of human civilisation. They longed for fresh water and food. At some point, their lucky cat dashed into the forest never to be seen again.

For the next few days, they travelled up the coast looking out for any signs of civilisation. Eventually they came across the Mapuche people, the indigenous people of Chile. The Mapuche people were very friendly, however they did not offer them any food but were able to tell them through hand gestures how far away Valdivia was. It was only another three leagues, which is roughly 10 miles. The men jumped back into the boat and pushed off, excited for the last leg of their journey.

Only a few hours later they rounded the bend and found themselves in the large, well-sheltered bustling Port of Valdivia. It had taken them roughly seven weeks and they had reached what looked to be a paradise with its crystal blue calm water, green pine trees with a backdrop of a rugged mountain range tucked behind the town. There were also small islands dotted about. To their surprise they were welcomed with open arms. Other boats sailed up to greet them and help them find the best spot to come ashore. A group of soldiers happily helped them carry their longboat onto the beach. The men felt a sense of joy, relief and excitement as they embarked on their new life with their new identities.

They settled into society as 10 gentlemen who had come from Liverpool on the *Mary* that had been shipwrecked on their way to Valparaiso. They gave themselves new names and James Porter even changed nationalities, becoming James O'Connor the Irishman. They told the Chileans a sorrowful story of the captain of their ship refusing to leave and going down with her. When the Chileans asked what their trades were, some said carpenters and others said they were sailors. So, the group was split up with the carpenters sent 10 miles upriver to the town centre where there was a great need for their skills and the five sailors went to Valparaiso. Everything was going better than they had expected until one of the carpenters got drunk on the journey up the river and made a slip-up. When they arrived in town, they were immediately escorted to holding cells where the Chileans began to interrogate them.

Meanwhile the sailors spent the evening having a great time partying on the beach until they woke up dazed and confused with soldiers pointing their guns at them. The men were briskly taken to the barracks where they were locked into cells. Under intense interrogation one of the convicts finally cracked. According to Porter it was Cheshire who gave a full confession to the Governor. Once the truth was out, they begged the Governor for clemency. The Governor was curious as to why they had chosen Chile and one of them replied, *'because we knew that you were patriots and had long ago declared your independence.'* The

Governor agreed to support their bid for freedom by trying to convince the Chilean Secretary of State for Foreign Affairs in Santiago. He did this with the condition that they do not attempt to escape. He then freed them under parole. They were not to leave Valdivia and had to report regularly to an officer. The men were both surprised and relieved.

The next few months were spent enjoying the fruits of Valdivian life. The men found employment, some working in the shipyards while others worked on government vessels. It wasn't long before some of the men got married, despite the fact that a few were already married with children. Their incredible story was published in the local paper and the people of Valdivia viewed them as legends. The fact that they had crossed the ocean in a leaky boat to escape their captors earnt them the respect and love of the local people. Somehow a copy of the newspaper article found its way into the hands of Governor Arthur of Van Diemen's Land. He had a very different view of the 10 convicts and wrote to England expressing the need to recapture the men.

Letters were sent and negotiations began between the Chilean Secretary of State for Foreign Affairs, Don Juaquin Tocornal and the British Vice-Consul in Valparaiso, Colonel John Walpole. Tocornal didn't want to give the convicts up. He knew that his people had embraced the men and there would be a public outcry if they were sent back to England. Plus, the men had displayed model behaviour in the months that they had been with them. He knew if they were sent back that they would probably be hanged for their crimes and that didn't sit well with him and his people. So, he bought time by demanding papers with all their information, noting that the piratical seizure wasn't surprising given the deplorable conditions that they had been subjected to in Van Diemen's Land. Walpole demanded they be imprisoned until their papers arrived from England, but this was denied.

The 10 convicts realised that they were on borrowed time, so Barker started looking for a way out. He propositioned a captain who had had his brig impounded for bringing in illicit cargo. He made an agreement that if he could secure his ship that the captain would give him and his mates passage to wherever they were sailing next. They waited for a moonless night and nine of the convicts (Cheshire was not included in this plan) slipped out of the town and sailed away. They were in two groups. There were the three Johns – Dady, Fare and Jones in one little sailboat and the six others were in a dinghy. The three Johns were easily able to get out to meet the ship, but the others were faced with a strong current and heavy onshore winds. They knew that they would never be able to get out to the ship and were forced to abandon the getaway. The three Johns left without them and were never seen again. It is thought that they sailed to Peru and eventually two of them went to America.

When Walpole learnt of their escape, he was furious. Fearful of Walpole's obsession with capturing them, Barker began a new plan of escape. He and some of the other men started building their own whaleboat under the pretence of making it for the Governor. When it was complete, Barker, Leslie and Russen quietly rowed it out on a very calm night and managed to pass the heads where they had got into trouble the last time and pushed out into the ocean. Barker left his wife and newborn child, and Leslie and Russen also left their wives behind.

The following morning when it was discovered that the three convicts were missing, the last four remaining men,

Porter, Cheshire, Shires and Lyon were locked up in the cells. They no longer had the Governor's protection as he had been replaced by a new Governor. Porter noted in his memoir, *'I then gave up hope of ever regaining my liberty'*. The men were chained together in pairs as letters went back and forth between the Chileans and the British. Months later a vessel was arranged to pick the four convicts up. Before it arrived, Porter made another attempt to escape by filing away at his leg irons and scaling the wall of the prison. He was soon caught and sent back. Right before Christmas in 1835 Leslie and Russen were also recaptured, but after bribing a guard, they managed to escape again.

By late April 1836 the last of the 10 *Frederick* men were escorted in chains onto HMS *Basilisk* and said goodbye to the freedom they had enjoyed for the past two years. They spent months travelling to different places, including back to England, and then were put on a ship to Hobart. A very close eye was kept on all of them out of fear that they may piratically seize the ship. The story of their capture of the *Frederick* had travelled and had taken on a life of its own. They were looked on in awe and fear. According to Porter's memoir, Lyon and Cheshire accused him and Shires of planning a mutiny and they were flogged mercilessly.

When they arrived in Hobart there was a new Governor in place. There they awaited their trial. Porter was still claiming to be an innocent man by the name of James O'Connor, however many in Hobart town knew his real identity. The trial began and ended within a month of their return. They were being charged on three counts. The first was piracy, the second and third were charges concerning the betrayal of trust as sworn mariners. Several witnesses were called, which included Mr Hoy the shipwright, James Tate the first mate, William Nicholls one of the convicts and others. All four men claimed not to have taken active parts in the mutiny and said they had only been following the other convicts out of fear. They repeatedly pointed out how they had not ill-treated their captives and had provided them with provisions. It was also raised as part of their defence that technically the *Frederick* had not been registered yet and could not therefore be seen as being piratically seized.

The jury took less than an hour and came back with a verdict of guilty, pointing out that they were of the opinion that the offence was not committed on the high seas, nor were they technically mariners. Justice Pedder noted '*the offense itself is a robbery not a piracy*'. Not knowing what to do with the men, their sentencing was suspended indefinitely. They lingered in prison for two years. The men had gained the sympathy of the public as they had not harmed anyone in the process of taking the *Frederick* and were just trying to escape a terrible and inhumane place. The case was debated in the Executive Council, and it was agreed that they should not face the death penalty but were to be transported for life to Norfolk Island.

James Porter was in and out of trouble for the rest of his life. Lyon too repeatedly reoffended but eventually received a pardon. William Shires spent some time in Newcastle then was awarded a Ticket of Leave and then a pardon for good conduct. William Cheshire committed a few minor offences which earnt him a trip back to Van Diemen's Land, but earnt himself a pardon in 1850. The other *Frederick* men were never heard of again, though there were many rumours about where they ended up.

Glossary

Absolute Pardon - A highly sought after piece of paper that restored a convict's freedom. They were given all their citizenship rights and allowed to leave the colony. They were permitted to return to the British Isles if they so chose. The first Absolute Pardon was issued in 1790 to a convict named John Irving.

Bilboes - An iron bar with sliding shackles and a padlock. It was most often attached around the ankles. The bilboe could be locked to the floor to prevent any chance of escape. They were commonly used at sea to prevent troublesome prisoners from roaming the ship.

Certificate of Freedom - This was awarded to a convict when they had completed their sentence. It was issued for the first time in 1810 in NSW. When a convict's sentence was complete they applied to a magistrate who checked their ship indent and issued the certificate when they were satisfied that the sentence had expired.

Conditional Pardon - This was awarded to convicts who had been given a life sentence. It released them from being a prisoner but all their rights were not restored. They were unable to leave the colony and return to the British Isles.

Fenian - A member of the 19th century revolutionary

nationalist group known as the Irish Republican Brotherhood.

Frost Fairs -Temperatures dropped so dramatically in London during the 'Little Ice Age' that the Thames would freeze over. Before 1814 the Thames was wider and shallower which caused it to freeze more easily. Out of work sailors and bargemen earnt money guiding people out onto the ice. Entrepreneurs set up markets on the frozen ice which became known as the Frost Fairs.

Japanned - Japanning is a type of finish consisting of a heavy, usually black, lacquer. It's an imitation of East Asian lacquerwork. It gained popularity in Europe in the late 17th century. At first it was used on furniture but then became popular on all sorts of materials especially metal objects. The technique of layering the resin base varnish applied in heat-dried layers, which are then polished, also rendered the item rustproof and was ideal for containers that carried water. Decoration layers were often made of gold painted leaves.

Jolly boat - A small wooden boat that ferried people to and from the ship. They were commonplace during the 18th and 19th centuries and were generally between 4.9m by 5.5m long and propelled by oars. When not in use they were strung up by davits to the stern of the ship and were hoisted in and out of the water when needed.

Pinnace - A light boat which was usually rowed but could be rigged with a sail. It was carried aboard large ships and used to run small errands such as ferry passengers, communicate between vessels and carry goods from shore.

Rosin - A pitch made from plant resin. It was often used to help caulk the seams of wooden sailing vessels, waterproof wooden containers and make torches.

Slop clothing - Cheaply made, loose clothing.

Ticket of Leave - Issued to convicts for good behaviour. It allowed a convict to work for themselves, but they were not to leave a specified area. They had to have their certificate on them at all times.

Whaleboat - A Long narrow open boat with sharp ends that could be operated with an oar or sail. They were designed for quick turning in rough seas and were roughly 20 to 30 feet long.

Bibliography

Amphitrite

Bateson, C. 1959, *The Convict Ships, 1787 – 1868*, Son & Ferguson, Ltd., Glasgow

Mawer, G.A. 1997, *Most Perfectly Safe: the convict shipwreck disasters of 1833-42*, Allen & Unwin, St Leonards NSW

Stone, G. 2009 *Beautiful Bodies: The Doomed Voyage of the Convict Ship Amphitrite and Her Cargo of Infamous Damned Whores*, Pan MacMillian, Sydney

The *Surry*

1788-1842 *New South Wales Government. Indents First Fleet, Second Fleet and Ships*. NRS 1150, microfiche 620–624. State Records Authority of New South Wales, Kingswood, New South Wales, Australia.

1813, *Trial of RICHARD ROBERTSON, THOMAS BLADE* (t18130217-44), Old Bailey Proceedings Online (version 8.0), viewed 4 Oct 2023, https://www.oldbaileyonline.org/browse.jsp?id=t18130217-44-defend421&div=t18130217-44#highlight

1814, *Sydney.*, The Sydney Gazette and New South Wales Advertiser (NSW : 1803 - 1842), 30 July, p. 2. , viewed 21 Jul 2023, http://nla.gov.au/nla.news-article628954 https://trove.nla.gov.au/newspaper/article/628954?searchTerm=SURRY

1814, *Classified Advertising*, The Sydney Gazette and New South Wales Advertiser (NSW : 1803 - 1842), 30 July, p. 1. , viewed 21 Jul 2023, http://nla.gov.au/nla.news-article628955

1814, *Classified Advertising*, The Sydney Gazette and New South Wales Advertiser (NSW : 1803 - 1842), 20 August, p. 1. , viewed 21 Jul 2023, http://nla.gov.au/nla.news-article628967

1815 *Sydney. SITTING MAGISTRATE-W. BROUGHTON, Esq.*, The Sydney Gazette and New South Wales Advertiser (NSW : 1803 - 1842), 28 January, p. 1. , viewed 21 Jul 2023, *http://nla.gov.au/nla.news-article629048*

Watson, F. & Chapman, P. & Australia. Parliament. Library Committee. 1914, Historical records of Australia Library Committee of the Commonwealth Parliament, Sydney viewed 4 October 2023 http://nla.gov.au/nla.obj-483306922

Bateson, C. 1959, *The Convict Ships, 1787 – 1868*, Son & Ferguson, Ltd., Glasgow

Ford, E. 1967, *Redfern, William* (1774–1833), Australian Dictionary of Biography, National Centre of Biography, Australian National University, viewed 29 Sep 2023, https://adb.anu.edu.au/biography/redfern-william-2580/text3533

Maud, H.E. 1967 *Raine, Thomas* (1793–1860), Australian Dictionary of Biography, National Centre of Biography, Australian National University, viewed 29 Sep 2023, https://adb.anu.edu.au/biography/raine-thomas-2570/text3511

Three Naked Convicts, a Kangaroo Suit and the Dog-Line

Lempriere, T.J 1796-1852, *The Penal Settlements of early Van Diemen's Land*, Royal Society of Tasmania, Northern Branch 1954, viewed 5 Oct 2023, https://viewer.slv.vic.gov.au/?entity=IE2021117&mode=browse

Old Bailey Proceedings Online version 8.0 1824, *Trial of GEORGE HUNT* (t18241028-107), viewed 24 Jul 2023, https://www.oldbaileyonline.org/browse.jsp?div=t18241028-107

1843 *Domestic Intelligence.*, Colonial Times (Hobart, Tas. : 1828 - 1857), 24 January, p. 3. , viewed 05 Oct 2023, http://nla.gov.au/nla.news-article8753277

1843 *REWARD!*, Launceston Advertiser (Tas. : 1829 - 1846), 26 January, p. 4. , viewed 29 Sep 2023, http://nla.gov.au/nla.news-article84767681

Cash, Martin. 1911, *Martin Cash, the bushranger of Van Diemen's Land in 1843-4 : a personal narrative of his exploits in the bush and his experiences at Port Arthur and Norfolk Island J. Walch & Sons*, Hobart, viewed 29 September 2023 *http://nla.gov.au/nla.obj-2595495428*

Maxwell-Stewart, H. & Hood, S. 2001, *Pack of Thieves? : 52 Port Arthur lives*, Port Arthur Historic Site Management Authority, Tasmania

Barnard, S. 2014, *A – Z of convicts in Van Diemen's Land*, Text Publishing, Melbourne, Victoria

Thomas Drewery, An Innocent Man

1847, The Hull Packet, and East Riding Times, 3 December, p. 4., viewed 26 Apr 2021, https://www.newspapers.com/image/390168750/?terms=thomas%20drewery&match=1

1847, *Thomas Drewery's Case*, The Hull Packet, and East Riding Times, 3 December, p. 4., viewed 26 Apr 2021, https://www.newspapers.com/image/390169776/?terms=thomas%20drewery&match=1

1847, *Thomas Drewery's Case*, The Hull Packet, and East Riding Times, 17

December, p. 5., viewed 26 Apr 2021, https://www.newspapers.com/image/390170814/?terms=thomas%20drewery&match=1

1847, *Transportation of an Innocent Man*, The Hull Packet, and East Riding Times, 24 December, p. 7., viewed 26 Apr 2021, https://www.newspapers.com/image/390171008

1848, *Thomas Drewery, The Innocent Convict,* The Hull Packet, and East Riding Times, 14 January, p. 5., viewed 26 Apr 2021, https://www.newspapers.com/image/390161646/

1848, *Thomas Drewery,* The Hull Packet, and East Riding Times, 21 January, p. 4., viewed 27 Apr 2021, https://www.newspapers.com/image/390161781/?terms=thomas%20drewery&match=1

1848, *Subscription for Thomas Drewery,* The Hull Packet, and East Riding Times, 28 January, p. 4., viewed 27 Apr 2021, https://www.newspapers.com/image/390161972/?terms=thomas%20drewery&match=1

1848, *Thomas Drewery*, The Hull Packet, and East Riding Times, 14 April, p. 5., viewed 27 Apr 2021, https://www.newspapers.com/image/390166342/?terms=thomas%20drewery&match=1

1848, *Thomas Drewery,* The Hull Packet, and East Riding Times, 28 April, p. 5., viewed 26 Apr 2021, https://www.newspapers.com/image/390169776/?terms=thomas%20drewery&match=1

1848, *Thomas Drewery,* The Hull Packet, and East Riding Times, 26 May, p. 5., viewed 27 Apr 2021, https://www.newspapers.com/image/390167742

Seal, G. 2017, *Great Convict Stories, Dramatic and moving tales from Australia's brutal early years,* Allen & Unwin

Small, D. 2020, *An Innocent Pentonvillain, Thomas Drewery, chemist and exile 1821-1859,* Public Record Office Victoria, viewed 5 Oct 2023, https://prov.vic.gov.au/explore-collection/provenance-journal/provenance-2015/innocent-pentonvillain

Convict Pirates of Moreton Bay

1827 *Supreme Criminal Court.*, The Sydney Gazette and New South Wales Advertiser (NSW : 1803 - 1842), 16 May, p. 2. , viewed 18 Apr 2023, http://nla.gov.au/nla.news-article2188226

1827 *Supreme Criminal Court.*, The Sydney Gazette and New South Wales Advertiser (NSW : 1803 - 1842), 4 June, p. 3. , viewed 18 Apr 2023, http://nla.gov.au/nla.news-article2188353

1832 *MORETON BAY.*, The Sydney Monitor (NSW : 1828 - 1838), 18 February, p. 4. (AFTERNOON), viewed 23 Apr 2023, http://nla.gov.au/nla.news-article32076948

1832 *Classified Advertising*, The Sydney Gazette and New South Wales Advertiser (NSW : 1803 - 1842), 1 March, p. 4. , viewed 25 Apr 2023, http://nla.gov.au/nla.news-article2205297

1832 *PIRACY.*, The Sydney Gazette and New South Wales Advertiser (NSW : 1803 - 1842), 17 May, p. 3. , viewed 24 Apr 2023, http://nla.gov.au/nla.news-article2206619

1832 *NARRATIVE*, The Sydney Herald (NSW : 1831 - 1842), 17 May, p. 2. , viewed 20 Apr 2023, http://nla.gov.au/nla.news-article12844491

1832 *CAPTAIN BROWNING'S NARRATIVE.*, Launceston Advertiser (Tas. : 1829 - 1846), 26 June, p. 8. , viewed 06 Oct 2023, http://nla.gov-.au/nla.news-article84773485

1887 *THE LATE CAPTAIN BROWNING.*, The Daily News (Perth, WA : 1882 - 1955), 25 August, p. 3. , viewed 25 Apr 2023, http://nla.gov.au/nla.news-article76068841

2019. *THE CONVICT PIRATES OF MORETON BAY – ON THE RUN IN THE SOUTH PACIFIC*, Moreton Bay and More, Stories from our past, Karen B, 5 May 2019, https://moretonbayandmore.com/2019/05/05/the-pirate-convicts-of-moreton-bay-part-2/

Australia's First Cold Case and the Man They Couldn't Hang

1803 *ROBBERY.*, The Sydney Gazette and New South Wales Advertiser (NSW : 1803 - 1842), 28 August, p. 4. , viewed 01 Aug 2021, http://nla.gov.au/nla.news-article625757

1803 *Third Day.*, The Sydney Gazette and New South Wales Advertiser (NSW : 1803 - 1842), 25 September, p. 3. , viewed 03 Aug 2021, http://nla.gov.au/nla.news-article625790

1803 *SYDNEY.*, The Sydney Gazette and New South Wales Advertiser (NSW : 1803 - 1842), 2 October, p. 2. , viewed 08 Aug 2021, http://nla.gov.au/nla.news-article625802

2012 *Joseph Luker.*, The Australian Police, viewed 04 Aug 2021, https://www.australianpolice.com.au/joseph-luker/?print=print

Franks, R. 2018 *The Murder of Joseph Luker.*, The Dictionary of Sydney, viewed 01 Aug 2021, https://home.dictionaryofsydney.org/the-murder-of-joseph-luker/

Franks, R. 2019, *The murder of Constable Joseph Luker*, Dictionary of Sydney, viewed 03 Aug 2021, http://dictionaryofsydney.org/entry/the_-murder_of_constable_joseph_luker

A Daring Escape from the Road Gangs of Western Australia

1869 *BUNBURY.*, The Inquirer and Commercial News (Perth, WA : 1855 -

1901), 13 January, p. 2. , viewed 21 Aug 2021, http://nla.gov.au/nla.news-article66033268

1870 *THE ESCAPE OF JOHN BOYLE O'REILLY.*, Advocate (Melbourne, Vic. : 1868 - 1954), 1 January, p. 13. , viewed 12 Aug 2021, http://nla.gov.au/nla.news-article170149320

1870 *J. BOYLE O'REILLY.*, Freeman's Journal (Sydney, NSW : 1850 - 1932), 26 February, p. 4. , viewed 12 Aug 2021, http://nla.gov.au/nla.news-article115292629

Pease, Z. W. 1897 *THE CATAPLA EXPEDITION.*, New Bedford, Mass: G.S. Anthony, viewed 16 Aug 2021, https://archive.org/details/catalpaexpeditio00peas/page/52/mode/2up

Birman, W. 2006 *O'REILLY, JOHN BOYLE (1844-1890)*, Australian Dictionary of Biography, viewed 5 September 2021, https://adb.anu.edu.au/biography/oreilly-john-boyle-4338

Kenneally, I. *John Boyle O'Reilly*, viewed 5 September 2021, https://www.johnboyleoreilly.com/convict.html

The Audacious Plot to Rescue Six Irish Convicts from Prison

1876 *FREMANTLE—PORT TOPICS.*, The Western Australian Times (Perth, WA : 1874 - 1879), 21 April, p. 2. , viewed 29 Aug 2021, http://nla.gov.au/nla.news-article2975872

1876 *DARING ESCAPE OF SIX FENIAN PRISONERS*, The Herald (Fremantle, WA : 1867 - 1886), 22 April, p. 3. , viewed 29 Aug 2021, http://nla.gov.au/nla.news-article109902454

1876 *ESCAPE OF FENIANS FROM SWAN HILL.*, The Burrangong Argus (NSW : 1865 - 1913), 14 June, p. 2. , viewed 25 Aug 2021, http://nla.gov.au/nla.news-article247273673

1876 (*To the Editors of the Protestant Standard.*), The Protestant Standard (Sydney, NSW : 1869 - 1895), 8 July, p. 2. , viewed 07 Sep 2021, http://nla.gov.au/nla.news-article207785686

1876 *EUROPEAN TELEGRAMS.*, The Colac Herald (Vic. : 1875 - 1918), 5 September, p. 3. , viewed 25 Aug 2021, http://nla.gov.au/nla.news-article91999619

1886 *THE END OF AN EXILE.*, Globe (Sydney, NSW : 1885 - 1886), 19 May, p. 8. (FIRST EDITION and EVENING), viewed 07 Sep 2021, http://nla.gov.au/nla.news-article102562460

Pease, Z. W. 1897 *THE CATAPLA EXPEDITION.*, New Bedford, Mass: G.S. Anthony, viewed 16 Aug 2021, https://archive.org/details/catalpaexpeditio00peas/page/52/mode/2up

The Disastrous Voyage of *George III*

1835 *The Courier.*, The Hobart Town Courier (Tas. : 1827 - 1839), 17 April, p. 2. , viewed 20 Oct 2021, http://nla.gov.au/nla.news-article4180760

1835 SHIPWRECK, The Hobart Town Courier (Tas. : 1827 - 1839), 24 April, p. 4. , viewed 26 Oct 2021, http://nla.gov.au/nla.news-article4180715

1872 *NARRATIVE OF THE WRECK OF THE GEORGE III. CONVICT SHIP.*, The Mercury (Hobart, Tas. : 1860 - 1954), 19 December, p. 2. (The Mercury Supplement), viewed 19 Oct 2021, http://nla.gov.au/nla.news-article8919451

Bateson, C. 1959, *The Convict Ships, 1787 – 1868*, Son & Ferguson, Ltd., Glasgow

Mawer, G.A. 1997, *Most Perfectly Safe: the convict shipwreck disasters of 1833-42*, Allen & Unwin, St Leonards NSW

2020 *Shipwreck – George III.*, Australasian Underwater Cultural Heritage Database., Department of Agriculture, Water and the Environment, viewed 30 Oct 2021, http://www.environment.gov.au/shipwreck/public/wreck/wreck.do?key=7195

The Tea Sweeteners

1832 *LAW INTELLIGENCE*, The Sydney Herald (NSW : 1831 - 1842), 21 May, p. 3. , viewed 12 Sep 2023, http://nla.gov.au/nla.news-article12844523

1832 *DIABOLICAL CONSPIRACY TO MURDER THE CREW AND GUARD OF THE GOVERNOR PHILIP TRANSPORT, ON HER PASSAGE TO NORFOLK ISLAND.*, The Sydney Gazette and New South Wales Advertiser (NSW : 1803 - 1842), 4 December, p. 2. , viewed 25 Jul 2021, http://nla.gov.au/nla.news-article2209731

1832 *DOMESTIC INTELLIGENCE. ABSTRACT OF SALES BY AUCTION.*, The Sydney Herald (NSW : 1831 - 1842), 6 December, p. 2. , viewed 25 Jul 2021, http://nla.gov.au/nla.news-article12845867

1832 *ARMY INTELLIGENCE.*, The Currency Lad (Sydney, NSW : 1832-1833), 8 December, p. 3. , viewed 25 Jul 2021, http://nla.gov.au/nla.news-article252636815

1833 *INDIA.*, Launceston Advertiser (Tas. : 1829 - 1846), 3 January, p. 424. , viewed 25 Jul 2021, http://nla.gov.au/nla.news-article84776276

1898 *THE STORY OF KNATCHBULL.*, The Australian Star (Sydney, NSW : 1887 - 1909), 2 April, p. 8. , viewed 25 Jul 2021, http://nla.gov.au/nla.news-article228431278

CONVICT AUSTRALIA

The First Fleeters and their Struggle for Food

Tench, W. 1759?-1833 & Flannery, T. F. 2000, *Two Classic Tales of Australian exploration: 1788, by Watkin Tench; Life and Adventures, by John Nicol*, edited & introduced by Tim Flannery, Text Publishing Company, Melbourne

Bateson, C. 1959, *The Convict Ships, 1787 – 1868*, Son & Ferguson, Ltd., Glasgow

Hill. D. 2010 *1788: The Brutal Truth of the First Fleet*, Random House Australia, North Sydney.

People Australia 2012-2023, *Barrett, Thomas (c. 1758-1788)*, National Centre of Biography, Australian National University, https://peopleaustralia.anu.edu.au/biography/barrett-thomas-30158/text37432, viewed 1 December 2021

Hill, D. 2015, *First Fleet Surgeon: the voyage of Arthur Bowes Smyth.*, National Library of Australia, Canberra, ACT

Royal Australian Historical Society 2021, *Jacqui Newling – Food in the first settlement of NSW 1788-1795*, https://www.youtube.com/watch?v=vu9mipK2VrQ, viewed 10 December 2021

The Sinking of the *Guardian*

1790, *Fortunate Escape of the Guardian Man of War, In her Voyage to Botany-Bay*, The Derby Mercury, Thursday, 29 April 1790, viewed 3 January 2022, www.newspapers.com/image/394415900

1790, *The Guardian*, The Public Advertiser, London, Friday, 30 April 1790, viewed 3 January 2022, www.newspapers.com/image/34415081

1790, *Guardian*, The Public Advertiser, London, Saturday, 1 May 1790, viewed 3 January 2022, www.newspapers.com/image/34415103

1790, Jacksons Oxford Journal, Saturday, 1 May 1790, viewed 3 January 2022, www.newspapers.com/image/396531048

1790, Ipswich Journal (Ipswich, Suffolk, England), Saturday, 1 May 1790, viewed 3 January 2022 www.newspapers.com/image/396394146 & www.newspapers.com/image/396394185

Lieut. Riou, Commander 1808, *Melancholy Disaster of His Majesty's Ship The Guardian, Bound to Botany Bay with Stores and Convicts*, London.

Hill, D. 2010 *1788: The Brutal Truth of the First Fleet.*, Random House Australia, North Sydney.

The Extraordinary Story of Mary Bryant – First Fleeter, Wife and Mother

Collins, D. 1756-1810 & Collier, J. 1910, *An Account of the English colony in New South Wales by David Collins 1756 - 1810*. Edited, with an introduction, and notes by James Collier, https://archive.org/details/b1182480/page/112/mode/2up, viewed 2 April 2022

Tench, W. 1759?-1833 & Flannery, T. F. 2000, *Two Classic Tales of Australian exploration: 1788, by Watkin Tench; Life and Adventures, by John Nicol*, edited & introduced by Tim Flannery, Text Publishing Company, Melbourne

Currey, C. H. 1963, *The Transportation, Escape and Pardoning of Mary Bryant (Nee Broad)*, Angus & Robertson Ltd, Sydney

Cameron, M. A. 2015, *Charlotte*, Dictionary of Sydney, http://dictionaryofsydney.org/entry/charlotte, viewed 19 May 2022

Hadfield, S. 2015-2016, *Convict Hulks*, Digital Panopticon, https://www.digitalpanopticon.org/Convict_Hulks, viewed 2 April 2022

Causer, T. 2017, *Memorandum of James Martin, An Astonishing Escape from Early New South Wales*, Edited by Tim Causer, UCL Press, United Kingdom.

The Cooking Pot Riot

1846 *NORFOLK ISLAND.*, The Sydney Morning Herald (NSW : 1842 - 1954), 8 August, p. 2. , viewed 11 May 2022, http://nla.gov.au/nla.news-article12889016

1846 *DISTURBANCES AT NORFOLK ISLAND.*, The Australian (Sydney, NSW : 1824 - 1848), 8 August, p. 3. , viewed 11 May 2022, http://nla.gov.au/nla.news-article37156047

1846 *Domestic Intelligence*, Colonial Times (Hobart, Tas. : 1828 - 1857), 25 August, p. 3. , viewed 11 May 2022, http://nla.gov.au/nla.news-article8759148

1846 *NORFOLK ISLAND.*, The Courier (Hobart, Tas. : 1840 - 1859), 2 September, p. 2. , viewed 28 May 2022, http://nla.gov.au/nla.news-article2944991

1846 *No Title*, The Hobart Town Advertiser (Tas. : 1839 - 1861), 4 September, p. 2. , viewed 25 May 2022, http://nla.gov.au/nla.news-article264517227

1846 *NORFOLK ISLAND.*, The Australian (Sydney, NSW : 1824 - 1848), 14 November, p. 3. , viewed 28 May 2022, http://nla.gov.au/nla.news-article37127840

1888 *CHAPTER OF OLD TIMES.*, Launceston Examiner (Tas. : 1842 - 1899), 12 June, p. 3. , viewed 28 May 2022, http://nla.gov.au/nla.news-article38316723

2005, *Westwood, William (1820–1846)*, M. Rutledge, Australian Dictionary of Biography, National Centre of Biography, Australian National University, viewed 29 May 2022, https://adb.anu.edu.au/biography/westwood-william-13246/text6635

Moore, J. 2011, *Alexander Maconochie's 'mark system.*, CORE: three access levels to underpin open access. D-Lib Magazine, viewed 28 May 2022, https://core.ac.uk/download/pdf/323897824.pdf

Casuer, T. 2021, *The Norfolk Island Penal Station, the Panopticon, and Alexander Maconochie's and Jeremy Bentham's Theories of Punishment*, Revue d'études benthamiennes [Online], viewed 28 May 2022, http://journals.openedition.org/etudes-benthamiennes/838

Neva - One of the Worst Shipwrecks in Australian History

1835 *MELANCHOLY SHIPWRECK.*, Launceston Advertiser (Tas. : 1829 - 1846), 2 July, p. 4. , viewed 23 Jan 2022, http://nla.gov.au/nla.news-article84777543

1835 *PARTICULARS OF THE WRECK OF THE Prison Ship "NEVA."*, The Sydney Monitor (NSW : 1828 - 1838), 18 July, p. 2. (MORNING), viewed 23 Jan 2022, http://nla.gov.au/nla.news-article32149374

1835 *Van Dieman's Land News.*, The Colonist (Sydney, NSW : 1835 - 1840), 23 July, p. 5. , viewed 23 Jan 2022, http://nla.gov.au/nla.news-article31716763

Bateson, C. 1959, *The Convict Ships, 1787 – 1868*, Son & Ferguson, Ltd., Glasgow

Mawer, G.A. 1997, *Most Perfectly Safe: the convict shipwreck disasters of 1833-42*, Allen & Unwin, St Leonards NSW

McCarthy, C. & Todd, K. & 2013, *The Wreck of the Neva, the horrifying fate of a convict ship and Irish women aboard* , Mercier Press, Australia

View Shipwreck – Neva, Australasian Underwater Cultural Heritage Database, viewed 18 June 2022, http://www.environment.gov.au/shipwreck/public/wreck/wreck.do?key=7542

Australia's First Bank Robbery

1828 *Classified Advertising*, The Sydney Gazette and New South Wales Advertiser (NSW : 1803 - 1842), 17 September, p. 1. , viewed 15 Jul 2022, http://nla.gov.au/nla.news-article2191066

1828 *EXTENSIVE ROBBERY AT THE BANK OF AUSTRALIA.*, The Sydney Gazette and New South Wales Advertiser (NSW : 1803 - 1842), 17 September, p. 2. , viewed 15 Jul 2022, http://nla.gov.au/nla.news-article2191067

1828 (*Domestic Intelligence continued.*), The Sydney Monitor (NSW : 1828 - 1838), 20 September, p. 4. (AFTERNOON), viewed 16 Jul 2022, http://nla.gov.au/nla.news-article31760702

1828 *Classified Advertising*, The Sydney Gazette and New South Wales Advertiser (NSW : 1803 - 1842), 22 September, p. 1. , viewed 16 Jul 2022, http://nla.gov.au/nla.news-article2191083

1828 *Classified Advertising*, The Sydney Gazette and New South Wales Advertiser (NSW : 1803 - 1842), 24 September, p. 3. , viewed 16 Jul 2022, http://nla.gov.au/nla.news-article2191099

1828 *Advertising*, The Australian (Sydney, NSW : 1824 - 1848), 24 September, p. 2. , viewed 16 Jul 2022, http://nla.gov.au/nla.news-article36865088

1828 *No title*, The Australian (Sydney, NSW : 1824 - 1848), 26 September, p. 2. , viewed 16 Jul 2022, http://nla.gov.au/nla.news-article36867843

1831 *Supreme Court.*, The Sydney Gazette and New South Wales Advertiser (NSW : 1803 - 1842), 14 June, p. 3. , viewed 25 Jul 2022, http://nla.gov.au/nla.news-article2201024

1833 *Government Gazette Notices*, New South Wales Government Gazette (Sydney, NSW : 1832 - 1900), 7 August, p. 302. , viewed 27 Jul 2022, http://nla.gov.au/nla.news-article230390571

Baxter, C. 2008, *Breaking the Bank, an extraordinary colonial robbery*, Allen & Unwin

Radford, N. 2017 *Robbing the Bank: Australia's First Bank Robbery*, Dictionary of Sydney, http://dictionaryofsydney.org/entry/robbing_the_bank_australias_first_bank_robbery, viewed 09 Aug 2022

Ten Convicts Seize the *Frederick*

1834 *ANOTHER GOVERNMENT VESSEL TAKEN BY HER GOVERNMENT CREW! ANOTHER SPECIMEN OF COLONEL ARTHUR'S PRISON DISCIPLINE.*, The Colonist and Van Diemen's Land Commercial and Agricultural Advertiser (Hobart Town, Tas. : 1832 - 1834), 11 February, p. 2. , viewed 11 Sep 2022, http://nla.gov.au/nla.news-article201158097

1834 *THE CONVICT SYSTEM. DARING ACT OF PIRACY*, The Sydney Herald (NSW : 1831 - 1842), 6 March, p. 2. , viewed 10 Sep 2022, http://nla.gov.au/nla.news-article12848817

1837 *SUPREME COURT.—CRIMINAL SITTINGS.*, Colonial Times (Hobart, Tas. : 1828 - 1857), 2 May, p. 5. , viewed 16 Sep 2022, http://nla.gov.au/nla.news-article8650013

Courtenay, A. 2018, *The Ship That Never Was, the greatest escape story of*

Australian colonial history., Harper Collins Publishers Australia Pty Limited

Drevikovsky, T & Williams, R. (Transcribers), *James Porter Autobiography, between 1840-1844,* Mitchell Library, State Library of New South Wales, viewed 16 Sep 2022, https://acms.sl.nsw.gov.au/_transcript/2013/D15087/a5629.htm

Acknowledgements

Thank you for reading my book!
If you enjoyed the book, please leave a review letting me know your thoughts. I would be delighted to hear from any descendants of the convicts within this publication.

I would also like to say thank you to my family and friends for their support and encouragement.

Jennifer Twemlow

Also by Jennifer Twemlow

Convict Sydney is a collection of biographies of the men, women and child convicts that were transported to Port Jackson between 1788 and 1840. It's not a compilation of the most successful or the worst offenders, but a medley of the everyday citizens that lived and breathed in Sydney town. Each character has been brought to life with glimpses into their personalities and their social lives, their hopes and aspirations. Their individual experiences offer a broader insight into the daily happenings of Sydney and the convict system. From Elizabeth Sullivan, who was known about town as the 'Fighting Hen of Cooks River' with her flamboyant dress and tough countenance, to Robert Sidaway who entertained local residents by hosting dramatic performances in his theatre.

We step into early Sydney as it was taking shape and learn about the types of work, routines, punishments, rewards, uniforms, marriage restrictions and so much more by walking in a convict's shoes. *Convict Sydney* also explores what life was like after the prisoners had completed their sentences. How they eked out a living and created their new identities in their tight-knit but ever growing community. Their stories flesh out the living reality.

Thought provoking, sometimes shocking, poignant and often uplifting, *Convict Sydney* offers both insight and entertainment as we become privy to the humanity of each convict, the highs and the lows of their lives.

www.ingramcontent.com/pod-product-compliance
Lightning Source LLC
Chambersburg PA
CBHW022015290426
44109CB00015B/1178